Praise for *Displaced in Gaza*

The testimonials in *Displaced in Gaza* are a record of choices that no human should be forced to make: to flee or to remain and die; to stay with loved ones or to bid them farewell. The narratives of these survivors of genocide are an affirmation of their humanity, an ode to loved martyrs, and a record with which to fight for future accountability and justice. It is an archive of enormous importance, yet one that is also lacking: there should be a testimony to each and every victim of Israeli apartheid. Every person in this collection is fighting back against the effort to make our loved ones nameless and silent, to leave their bodies unidentified beneath rubble. They are forcing us to witness, to hold their stories as a living archive against this latest act of extermination, as well as the years upon years of Nakba, of the dispossession and murder that preceded it.

—**Tareq Baconi**
*President of the board of Al-Shabaka,
the Palestinian Policy Network*

There will come a day, after this genocide, when Palestine is free, when many will claim they were unaware of the crimes that Israel, with the full backing of the United States, was perpetrating against the Palestinian people. These testimonies, given by Palestinians, in the midst of unimaginable atrocities and losses, bear witness in real time to what Israel has done. No one can ever claim they did not know.

—**Ali Abunimah**
*Cofounder of the Electronic Intifada and
author of* The Battle for Justice in Palestine

Displaced in Gaza presents an essential collection of real-life testimonies that challenge the narratives justifying the current erasure of Gaza and its people. In the Gaza Strip, where nine in ten Palestinians have been displaced since the events of October 7 – some as many as ten times – these personal accounts humanize the staggering numbers. These stories remind us of our shared responsibility to ensure that the lessons of history and the pledge of "never again for anyone" apply to Palestinians as well.

—**Laila Mokhiber**
Senior Director of Communications at UNRWA USA

Despite the immense anguish, pain, and suffering every author shares, they pale in comparison to the resilience and strength of every Palestinian who continues to pursue freedom and autonomy from their cruel oppressors. Hope and faith have become so deeply embedded within the Palestinian psyche that it is now part of their DNA. But, will children robbed of their childhood, and youths who know only fear and anger, be able to live well-adjusted lives in adulthood? The answer is clear – No. *Displaced in Gaza* serves as a document to remind the world not to forget or become immune to this insane and senseless war, and lend whatever assistance possible to help the country heal.

—**Musa Mohd Nordin**
Viva Palestina Malaysia

Displaced in Gaza is a must-read for those who want to understand the immense sufferings of the Palestinians as a result of the failure of the international community to stop the ongoing Zionist crime of ethnic cleansing in Palestine.

—**Professor Nazari Ismail**
Chairman of BDS Malaysia

Displaced in Gaza
Stories from the Gaza Genocide

Edited by
Yousef M. Aljamal
Norma Hashim
Noor Nabulsi
and Zoe Jannuzi

Haymarket Books
Chicago, IL

© Norma Hashim
First published by the Biblio Press Enterprise, Selangor, Malaysia

This edition published in 2025 by
Haymarket Books
P.O. Box 180165
Chicago, IL 60618
773-583-7884
www.haymarketbooks.org
info@haymarketbooks.org

ISBN: 979-8-88890-520-3

Cover art, *Traveling While Palestinian* © Mary Hazboun
maryhazboun.com

Distributed to the trade in the US through Consortium Book Sales and Distribution (www.cbsd.com) and internationally through Ingram Publisher Services International (www.ingramcontent.com).

This book was published with the generous support of Lannan Foundation, Wallace Action Fund, and the Marguerite Casey Foundation.

Special discounts are available for bulk purchases by organizations and institutions. Please email info@haymarketbooks.org for more information.

Printed in Canada by union labor.

Library of Congress Cataloging-in-Publication data is available.
Library of Congress Control Number: 2025938102

2 4 6 8 10 9 7 5 3 1

*Dedicated to all who have
endured displacement
in Gaza,
past and present.*

Displaced in Gaza is a collection of personal testimonies from Palestinians in Gaza who have been repeatedly displaced within their homeland since October 7, 2023. These testimonies were collected in May 2024, commissioned by the Hashim Sani Center for Palestine Studies at Universiti Malaya. *Displaced in Gaza* aims to raise global awareness about the violent and forced displacement inflicted upon Palestinians in Gaza by the Israeli military and the impact that this displacement has had on every aspect of their lives. Each story is unique, yet the endurance of the Palestinian people remains a common thread, linking together these stories of hope and loss.

Contents

Foreword
Ahmad Alnaouq — xi

Introduction
Yousef Aljamal — 1

Caring for Two Orphaned Children in Gaza
Aisha Osama Abu Ajwa — 5

I Lost My Son, My Support in This Life
Fidaa Fathi Abu Yousef — 11

Israel Killed Ten Members of My Family in One Airstrike
Rehab Musa Aljamal — 16

The Occupation Killed My Grandchildren and Dispersed My Family
Yusra Salem Abu Awad — 20

I Lost My Beautiful Father at 12 Years Old
Youssef Qawash — 25

Three Days Without Food or Water
Fatima Ahmed Abu Bakra — 29

My Husband Was Martyred, and There Is No Body: My Story of Pain Caused by the Israeli Occupation
Somia Issa Mustafa Saleh — 34

The Occupation Arrested My Sick Husband and We Live in Constant Suffering
Shaymaa Al-Eisswei — 39

The Occupation Killed My Husband and Left Me with
Our Three Children
Shaymaa Al-Durra   43

The Stolen Childhood of Palestinian Children
Saeed Al-Halabi   48

Over 100 Displaced People Have Sheltered in
My Home Since the Beginning of the War
Rasmiyya Ahmed Abbas   53

My Mother Returned Home to Die:
The Injustices Against Elderly Patients in the Gaza Strip
Ali Al-Owisi   60

The Need to Obtain Water Is the Greatest Suffering
We Are Exposed to in the Displacement Tents
Nidaa Abu Toha   65

My Husband Was Martyred While Searching for Food for Us
Najlaa Al-Kafarna   70

The Occupation Killed Every Member of My Family by
Bombing Our Home
Mohammed Ali Al-Bibi   76

Displaced in 1948 and Today, Surviving Another Nakba
and Genocide
Mohammed Abdul Jabbar Abu Seif   82

Under Siege in Khan Younis
Manar Wadi   88

Teaching 200 Children in Displacement Camps:
How I Turn Displacement Tents into Schools
Ikram Talaat Ahmed   93

Today, I Sell Chips, but Tomorrow, I Will Be a Doctor
Aseel Al Hawajri   98

Widowed on the Fifth Day of the War
Fidaa Al-Shakhreet   103

Israel Killed My Daughter on Her Third Birthday
Tareq Fareed Al Hajj   108

Creating Joy Despite Displacement
Akram Abdul Nabi Al-Ajrami   113

Providing Medical Services Under Impossible Conditions
Ahmed Nasr Halas   118

Raising My Martyred Son's Children
Nasreen Naeem Al-Hilu   123

The Israeli Occupation Steals the Dreams
of Palestinian Students
Mohammed Altaweel   128

Birth and Death Under Israeli Bombs
Hajj Abu Sultan   134

Only My Brother and I Survived the Bombing of Our Home
Hala Adel Al-Najmi   140

Remember Us
Paul Catafago   145

Acknowledgments   150

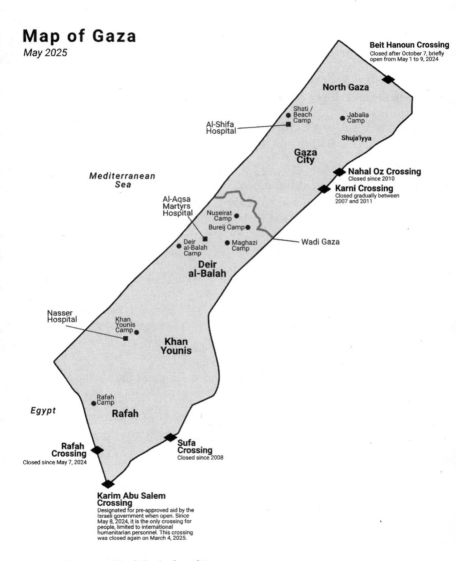

Foreword

Israel's forced displacement of Palestinians is not new. It did not begin during this ongoing genocide in Gaza; since the Nakba in 1948, it has been the defining feature of the Palestinian struggle and existence. It's been more than 76 years now since the Nakba, and the Palestinian people are still living in exile and displacement, both inside and outside their homeland. The 700,000 Palestinians who were forced to flee their homes and lands due to the ethnic cleansing enforced by Israel in 1948 now constitute the majority of the residents of the Gaza Strip and refugee camps in Lebanon, Jordan, Syria, and elsewhere. But the displacement of Palestinians didn't end in 1948; it has continued and is still ongoing.

From the crowded refugee camps of Lebanon, to the Yarmouk camp in Syria, to Jordan, the Gaza Strip, and the West Bank, displaced Palestinians have been at the forefront of the liberation movement of Palestine. They have led the way with courage, resilience, and an unwavering commitment to justice.

Within the confines of refugee camps and amid displacement, the powerful works of Palestinian authors and intellectuals have reflected the endurance and steadfastness of the Palestinian people and their devotion to their homeland. Legendary Palestinian author Ghassan Kanafani, born in Acre and displaced to Lebanon, is immortalized in his works like *Men in the Sun* and *Returning to Haifa*. Written during his exile, these works explore themes of identity, loss, and the might of the Palestinian people. Mahmoud Darwish, another noted Palestinian poet of exile and resistance, was born in al-Birwa and gained international acclaim with collections such as *Why Did You Leave the Horse Alone?* Samih al-Qasim, a native of Zarqa and a resident of Israel and the occupied Palestinian territories, wrote poignant poetry about resistance and identity in his book *Sadder Than Water* among other works. Fadwa Tuqan, the "poet of Palestine" from Nablus, captured the pain of exile in her collection *Alone With the Days*. Ibrahim Nasrallah, born in the Wihdat refugee camp in Jordan, chronicled Palestinian history and struggles in his novel *The Time of White Horses*.

Despite the hardships of displacement, these intellectuals have kept the flame of Palestinian identity alive. They not only inspired future generations, but also inked the history of Palestinians in exile and paved the way for this generation to follow suit.

Now, Gaza, my home, finds itself at the epicenter of genocide again – facing ethnic cleansing by means of the same practices that claimed the lives and properties of our grandparents in 1948, but with far more abhorrent crimes. During this genocide, I've lost most of my immediate family members – my father, two brothers, three sisters, and my 14 nieces and nephews, all children. As I write this, the *Lancet* medical journal has estimated that the death toll could exceed 186,000 Palestinians, all having lost their lives directly and indirectly from the merciless machinery of Israeli barbarism. Palestinians in Gaza find themselves once again forced to live displaced within the world's largest open-air prison. More than 90% of Gaza's population has been forced to evacuate from their homes and lands.

During the ethnic cleansing of the Nakba 76 years ago, Palestinians took it upon themselves to immortalize their stories, documenting these massacres in writing. But the old did not die, and the young did not forget, as Zionist leaders wrongly assumed they would. Palestinians, within the confines of their prison in Gaza, are once again writing their stories and recording history. The importance of Palestinians writing their own stories cannot be overstated. In a world where our voices are too often marginalized or misrepresented, storytelling becomes an act of resistance, a declaration of our humanity. Through our words, we reclaim our narrative, ensuring that our experiences are not only heard, but felt by those who might never understand the true cost of dispossession.

For more than ten months of this genocide, Palestinians in Gaza have spoken out from the crowded alleyways of makeshift refugee camps and the hospitals and schools used as shelters. Palestinians are writing their stories, documenting both the horror of the war and the resilience of the people. Everyone in Gaza is now a citizen journalist, determined more than ever to confront and challenge the western media narrative – the demonizing and dehumanizing of the Palestinians, the lack of agency recognized, and the distortion of truth. Young people and Gaza elders are recording testimonies – narrating their stories for the world to read.

In the face of such overwhelming adversity, the act of storytelling becomes a lifeline, a means of asserting our humanity and preserving our narrative. It is through the power of writing that we can transcend the constraints of our circumstances and connect with others on a profound level. The stories in this collection are not merely accounts of suffering; they are expressions of resilience, hope, and the unbreakable bond that ties us to our homeland. The process of writing and sharing these stories has been a deeply cathartic experience for the authors. It has allowed them to confront their pain, find solace in the practice of writing, and contribute to a collective memory that will endure for generations. Each story is a testament to the indomitable spirit of the Palestinian people. The stories are a declaration that we will not be defined by our suffering, but by our strength, our creativity, and our commitment to resist the occupation by every means possible.

In 2015, I cofounded We Are Not Numbers (WANN) on the belief that every Palestinian has a story worth telling. Our mission is to provide a platform for these stories, to amplify the voices of those who have been silenced, and to challenge the dominant narratives that seek to dehumanize us. Through the work of WANN, other writers, and multiple Palestinian-led platforms, Palestinians strive to create a more just and equitable world, one where the rights and dignity of all people are respected and upheld. Palestinians are now writing stories that reflect a range of experiences, from the everyday struggles of life under occupation, starvation, and genocide to the moments of joy and hope that sustain us and make us feel alive. They are stories of loss and longing, of courage and resilience, of dreams deferred but never abandoned.

Palestinians now understand the power of narrative in challenging the dominant discourses that seek to dehumanize us. Storytelling helps to assert our right to be seen and heard. Palestinian storytellers work tirelessly to ensure that our voices are centered and our experiences acknowledged and respected. We don't write to amuse our readers with fantasy epics or imaginary stories. We write in a language that is not ours to challenge perceptions imposed by our oppressors, ignite the empathy of our fellow human beings, and inspire others to stand in solidarity with the Palestinian people. Our stories are a call to action, a plea for justice, and a reminder that our shared humanity transcends the divisions that seek to separate us. *We write so that others cannot say they did not know.*

This book is a tribute to the memory of all those we have lost – the 21 members of my own family, killed by the Israeli army while they were sleeping; the thousands of students who lost their lives; the journalists and hundreds of academics taken away from their families at the hands of the occupiers; and most importantly, to Refaat Alareer, our mentor and hero.

I want to express my deepest gratitude to the Palestinians in Gaza who have shared their stories with such courage and honesty. Your voices are powerful, and your words have the ability to change hearts and minds. Through your stories, you are contributing to a legacy of resilience and hope. This anthology serves as a testament to our enduring spirit, a reminder that even in the face of displacement and adversity, we have the power to write, to dream, and to imagine a better world. A world without chains and walls, where writers and storytellers can not only live safely, but most importantly, in dignity. A life that we deserve.

Ahmad Alnaouq, July 2024

Introduction

Displaced in Gaza is a collection of testimonies by 27 Palestinians from Gaza who were forcibly displaced after October 7, 2023. In this crucial book, the American Friends Service Committee (AFSC) and the Hashim Sani Center for Palestine Studies (HSCPS) at Universiti Malaya bring these testimonies to life. This book intends to uplift the voices of Palestinians in Gaza during this tragic moment in history, when Gaza has been subjected to a genocide and the world has turned its back on it. This book contributes to the project of documenting first-hand the narratives of Palestinians who have lived through a genocide which began in October 2023 and continues as this introduction is being written.

These 27 Palestinians include students, mothers, fathers, grandparents, survivors of the 1948 Nakba, children, and educators. The book intentionally represents the stories of a diverse group of Palestinians in Gaza. But although the stories are diverse, they are laced together by themes of grief, hardship, and hope for a better future. Students in the book are deprived of their education, mothers are deprived of their motherhood, and fathers are left helplessly watching their children suffer.

Displaced in Gaza shows us that the Nakba never ended. Though most in Gaza are displaced, the burden of displacement falls especially hard on Nakba survivors who are forced to relive the experiences of displacement, destruction, and death.

This project is a commitment to storytelling, a tradition which many Palestinians in Gaza have practiced, including Refaat Alareer. Refaat, a Palestinian poet and intellectual, visited the United States in 2014 as part of the *Gaza Writes Back* speaking tour, which was co-organized by the AFSC. The AFSC has a long history in Gaza, beginning with its establishment of refugee camps for Palestinians fleeing the Nakba in 1948. The United Nations took over the camps after establishing the United Nations Relief and Works Agency (UNRWA).

Refaat was also a non-resident scholar at the Hashim Sani Center for Palestine Studies and held many of his training workshops on writing and storytelling at the Hashim Sani Library in Gaza.

For centuries, Palestinians have tended the rich oral history of Palestine, preserving cultural heritage, including folktales and stories about the land. There is a constant need to tell the stories of people in Gaza. *Displaced in Gaza* documents the displacement experience of dozens of Palestinians. The book reminds us that there are 2.3 million Palestinians in Gaza who have been subjected to starvation, mass destruction, targeted killing, scholasticide, and severe mental health crises.

You will read the story of Fatima Ahmed Abu Bakra. She cares for her grandchildren and her remaining deaf children in a tent, as her home was leveled by the Israeli military. She became a refugee in 1948 at the age of four. At 80 years old, she dreams of the liberation of her homeland and her return.

You will read 12-year-old Saeed Al-Halabi's story of operating a trampoline business to provide entertainment for fellow displaced children in an UNRWA school in Nuseirat. He works long hours every day, earning a little money to support his family. Although he is happy to provide relief for traumatized children, he fears being killed by Israeli bombs everyday, especially after his cousin and many friends and neighbors were killed. The story of Al-Halabi is one example of how the childhoods of Gaza youth have been stolen.

The stories in *Displaced in Gaza* are not only about death. Educators continue to teach under impossible conditions. The story of Ikram Talaat Ahmed highlights the value Palestinians place on education in Gaza and the dedication they have for raising an educated generation. Before the genocide, Ikram worked as an English teacher and owned her own tutoring business. Now, her home and teaching center are rubble. Some of the teachers she employed were killed. Despite this loss, she teaches 200 children in her tent every day to send a message to the world that investment in education will always be the way forward for Palestinians.

Tareq Fareed Al Hajj speaks of the agony of losing his daughter to whom he promised a birthday party. Instead, Suwar, his daughter, was killed on her third birthday, along with her five-year-old sister. Their killings left their parents with broken hearts. The intensity of the bombing threw their light bodies far away from their home. Tareq writes, "I searched for my daughters for a long time, lifting rubble and stones with my hands. . . . I spoke to them, but they didn't respond. I quickly took them to the hospital, praying to God all the way that they would be alive, but when I arrived at Al-Aqsa Hospital, the doctors informed me that they had been killed due to the bombing."

Gaza's wounds are too fresh and deep. Palestinians in Gaza, including pharmacists, provide whatever medicine they can find to their patients. Ahmed Nasr Halas worked as a pharmacist and owned two pharmacies in Gaza City, both of which were bombed by Israel. He eventually opened a pharmacy in the displacement tent where he lives, and provides injections and medication to displaced people in need. He dreams of rebuilding his two pharmacies, opening a pharmaceutical company, and completing his master's and doctoral studies.

Ahmed does what Gaza needs the most today: healing. I hope the stories in *Displaced in Gaza* will provide you with a solid knowledge of life in Gaza but also deepen your understanding of the catastrophic situation. Understanding Gaza's reality is the first step to providing solutions that will enable Palestinians to live in dignity on their land. Rebuilding Gaza's health and educational institutions is a must. Before this most recent war, the health system was largely dependent on Israel approving the entry of medications and medical devices into Gaza, as well as granting

Palestinians in Gaza permits to travel for medical care in the West Bank. When Gaza is rebuilt, this reality should not exist again.

UNRWA's system of free education has helped keep Palestinians in Gaza well educated. They know what they want. Reconstruction efforts should center Palestinian demands and needs. These plans should be independent from Israel's desire to interfere in Palestinian schools' systems as it did in the West Bank.

In *Displaced in Gaza*, Palestinians speak of their aspirations and dreams. It is our job in turn to materialize these hopes and dreams in a way that empowers Palestinians. The stories in *Displaced in Gaza* make one important thing clear: the time to act is now.

Yousef Aljamal, July 2024

Caring for Two Orphaned Children in Gaza

Aisha Osama Abu Ajwa

❝ I screamed at the soldiers and raised my hands for them to stop. They pulled the child out of the pit, and we continued our journey of death among the merciless occupation's armored vehicles. ❞

I USED to live in Zaytoun neighborhood in the southeast of Gaza City with my husband, Kamal Abu Zour, and our four children in our home safely and peacefully. My husband's parents and his married siblings also lived with us in the same house. We lived together as a happy Palestinian family, sharing everything between us. But during this war, we shared pain in an indescribable way.

After the birth of my fourth son, my husband and I agreed to be content with the children that God had blessed us with, so we focused on raising our four children. The requirements of life are very demanding. We could barely provide for their needs to secure a decent life for them. But in this war, the crimes of the occupation added two orphaned children for me to care for and nurture after the occupation killed their parents. I am now a mother of six children.

During the last day of the temporary ceasefire at the end of November 2023, when Israeli prisoners were released in exchange for Palestinian prisoners, we lived on edge. We feared the return of the war.

My husband's sister-in-law and my friend Iman Salah Abu Zour went to visit and check on her family two days after the temporary ceasefire ended. She expected the temporary ceasefire to be extended, so she took her children with her: Rayan Ahmed Abu Zour, seven years old, Abdul Rahman, three years old, Adam, four years old, and Kan'an, one-and-a-half years old. My friend Iman was eager to see her mother, father, and siblings, as she hadn't seen them for over 50 days of the Israeli war on the Gaza Strip. Shortly after she arrived at her family's house on December 3, 2023, the Israeli forces bombed the entire residential block, killing Iman and her children Adam and Kan'an. Her children Rayan and Abdul Rahman were seriously injured.

Rayan and Abdul Rahman stayed in the intensive care unit for several days. Rayan was wounded with shrapnel all over his body and had third-degree burns on his right leg. The shrapnel is still lodged in his body. Abdul Rahman, or "Aboud" as we like to call him, was wounded with shrapnel in his head and remained in a coma for a week.

The children's injuries were severe, and I prayed to God at all times for their safety, as they are the remaining children of their young father, Ahmed, who lost his wife and two of his kids. After their wounds healed slightly, I took them to live in my house with my children. I love them, and my children love them. We used to live together in one house, each with our own apartment, but today, they are just like my own children.

The two children, Rayan and Abdul Rahman, have not recovered from the shock of losing their mother and siblings, and the wounds that the occupation inflicted upon them have not fully healed.

Three months after the martyrdom of their mother and siblings, on February 20, 2024, the occupation forces suddenly stormed the area of the Zaytoun neighborhood, besieging us in our homes amid heavy gunfire.

We couldn't leave our homes due to the intensity of the Israeli shelling. The bombardment and gunfire were indiscriminate and intense in our area. Quadcopter aircrafts fired at anyone who moved or tried to leave the area. The occupation forces advanced, blowing up the doors of houses and storming brutally into homes.

I tried to calm the six children, but all my attempts failed due to the severity of the violent shelling and relentless gunfire. The sounds of explosions drowned out all my attempts to calm them. My husband, Kamal Abu Zour, and several other young men, including his brother Ahmed, the father of the two children, were arrested and taken to an unknown location. We remained in the house, waiting for our turn to be killed or arrested.

The shock to the orphaned children, Rayan and Abdul Rahman, was immense. The occupation had arrested their father, Ahmed Ayyash Abu Zour, in front of their eyes. We were afraid for their fate, screaming for them not to be killed. We didn't know what would happen to them. Later, I learned of their father's martyrdom during his arrest.

The occupation forces stormed our house and asked us to leave. They allowed us to go out, but they prevented me from taking a bottle of water for the children. I wanted to grab my small child's bag with supplies and diapers, but they stopped me from taking it. I walked out of the house amid soldiers and tanks, holding on to the six children, not knowing where to escape with them.

The occupation forces asked me to walk on Salah al-Din Street toward the central and southern areas of the Gaza Strip. We left our house after being besieged by the occupation forces for several hours. I walked with the six children on foot among the tanks, occupation vehicles, and soldiers, with the relentless shelling continuing for over 15 kilometers [9.3 miles].

We had no food or water, and fear gripped the children's hearts in an indescribable manner. I screamed and cried, begging the soldiers to stop firing, but the shelling intensified. I walked with difficulty due to extreme fear. The children witnessed dozens of martyrs' bodies strewn on the ground. They cried intensely, while blood covered the streets.

The children asked for water, but I had nothing with me. We walked beside one of the tanks, which was moving quickly. The child Abdul Rahman fell into a pit by the road, just one meter away from the tank. I screamed at the soldiers and raised my hands for them to stop. They pulled the child out of the pit, and we continued our journey of death among the merciless occupation's armored vehicles.

I walked with the six children from the Zaytoun neighborhood to the Nuseirat refugee camp, a distance of about 15 kilometers. I carried the six children, including my youngest, a seven-month-old, and the eldest, Rayan, who is seven years old. The weather was extremely cold. When I reached the entrance of the Nuseirat camp, I screamed at the top of my lungs, "Where am I?" People told me that I was in the Nuseirat camp. We drank salty water, and I fed the children bread and lentils provided by the people of Nuseirat. We survived death that night, but Rayan and Abdul Rahman lost their father, a martyr.

I wandered on the street in the Nuseirat refugee camp in the Gaza Strip, waiting for my husband Kamal and his brother Ahmed, the father of the two children Rayan and Abdul Rahman. Then, the people of Nuseirat offered me and my family a place to stay in a small shop. Later, I learned that my husband had arrived at a school belonging to the United Nations Relief and Works Agency (UNRWA), in the middle of the camp. When my husband arrived at the school, he was only wearing underwear and was barefoot. A group of men, including my husband, had been arrested by the occupation forces for several hours, stripped of all their clothes, and interrogated. Then they were thrown onto the street.

The six children and I headed to the school and reunited with my husband on February 21, 2024. We arrived at the school center without clothes, shoes, food, or water. We had no permanent shelter; we had lost everything. I wandered the school looking for a place to sleep until I found a space in one of the classrooms. We slept on only a blanket and mattress on the floor. The living, health, and environmental conditions in the school were extremely difficult. We had no shelter of our own; we had lost everything.

My husband told me that the occupation forces killed his brother Ahmed, the father of the two children Rayan and Abdul Rahman, in front of his eyes. The occupation forces interrogated my husband and his brother, but then released them. As they were leaving the area of the occupation vehicles, the occupation forces fired directly at them. Ahmed was shot in the foot and abdomen. He was martyred on Salah al-Din Street in the passage that the occupation claimed was safe. My husband tried to retrieve his body, but the occupation forces fired at him. Ahmed's body remained lying on the ground among the occupation vehicles until stray dogs devoured it.

I have been living for three months in a school for displaced persons in the Nuseirat camp in the middle of the Gaza Strip. I live on three small mattresses with my six children. They are my sons Murad, six years old; Karam, five years old; Anas, four years old; Adi, seven months old; and the orphaned children Rayan, seven years old, and Abdul Rahman, three years old.

Rayan and Abdul Rahman are still suffering from their injuries sustained in the shelling that killed their mother and siblings. Shrapnel is still lodged in Rayan's head and face. He also has burns on his right foot. The shrapnel has not been removed from his body due to poor health conditions and the continuation of the war on the Gaza Strip. Abdul Rahman also suffers from a skull fracture, fluid in the testicles, constantly high blood sugar, and pain all over his body. All of my children suffer from difficulty sleeping and involuntary urination while sleeping due to the intense fear that still haunts them to this day.

Abdul Rahman suffers from severe psychological trauma and has emotional breakdowns when he hears his mother's name. The two children have become orphans, with no support. They have no one in this life except me. The occupation deprived them of their mother's affection and their father's care. The occupation forced them to continue their lives while injured, without any support.

Now, I am the mother of six children. The war has forced all of us to live in shelter centers. I hope the war ends soon, and we return to our home. We don't know if our house was destroyed or damaged. We just want the war to stop and to return to our lives before the war. ♦

I Lost My Son, My Support in This Life

Fidaa Fathi Abu Yousef

> ❝ I was terrified for my children, and we all began to sleep in one room. I used to tell them that if the house was bombed, we would die together, and if we survived, we would survive together. ❞

WHEN God blessed me with my first son, Odai, I embraced him and wished for him a successful life. I hoped he would complete his education, and find a job that would enable him to serve his community, country, and religion.

My name is Fidaa Fathi Abu Yousef. I am 40 years old, and

live in Nuseirat camp in the middle of the Gaza Strip. I graduated with a diploma in business administration from the Islamic University of Gaza in 2004. Nearly 20 years ago, I married Imad Al-Awdat and gave birth to four children: Odai, 18 years old; Raghad, 17 years old; Mohammed, 16 years old; and Leen, 11 years old. Until our separation in 2018, we lived in a house in Bureij camp.

After separating from my husband, I moved back into my father's house in Nuseirat camp. Here, I lived with my children in a small room that contained the kitchen, bathroom, and a place where all five of us slept.

We lived in this small apartment for over four years. I searched for a long time to find a job opportunity to improve my children's living conditions, but I couldn't find any. There are barely any jobs in the Gaza Strip, and unemployment rates are very high.

Several years ago, I thought of preparing and baking flatbread over a fire, which my son Odai would sell in the market. I brought my idea to life and managed to attract some customers — small restaurant owners. The work was sporadic and challenging, requiring considerable time and effort. My children helped me, and we were happy because this job provided us with an opportunity to improve our living conditions.

In September 2023, I managed to rent an apartment close to my family's house. My son Odai started high school in September 2023, and I was determined to provide a suitable atmosphere for him to study. We were happy in our new apartment. Though we rented it for 450 Israeli shekels every month, we had our own kitchen, bathroom, and three rooms.

The Israeli war on the Gaza Strip began on October 7, 2023, less than a month after we moved into the new apartment on the fourth floor. I feared for my children due to intense bombardment. Occupation forces bombed several houses adjacent to us, and dozens of our friends, neighbors, and loved ones were martyred. I was terrified for my children, and we all began to sleep in one room.

I LOST MY SON, MY SUPPORT IN THIS LIFE | 13

I used to tell them that if the house was bombed, we would die together, and if we survived, we would survive together.

Our financial situation deteriorated greatly during the war. The closure of all restaurants and crossings caused all Gaza Strip residents to lose their jobs and depleted food supplies from the markets. I lost my temporary job due to restaurant closures. We couldn't even find flour to cook with. The days were extremely difficult.

My son Odai searched for work in many areas, and on Wednesday, November 15, 2023, he found a job at one of the wood-fired bakeries in Nuseirat camp. I asked him to take care of himself and stay away from bombing sites. He was my eldest son, my friend and companion. After I separated from their father, he cared for his siblings. He meant everything to us.

Odai worked alongside our neighbors' sons. While transporting bread on his bicycle, Israeli forces bombed several residential apartments in the Salah Towers, south of Nuseirat camp. Odai was riding his bike under the tower when rubble from the bombing fell on his small body, instantly martyring him.

Neighbors' daughters informed me that Israeli forces had bombed the Salah Towers area, very close to Odai's new job. I rushed to the bombing site, about 800 meters from my house, searching for Odai but couldn't find him. I searched everywhere meticulously.

I hurried to Al-Awda Hospital in Nuseirat camp, searching among the injured for Odai, but I couldn't find him. I examined the faces of martyrs closely, searching for my son. Fear and tears overwhelmed me. I wanted my son. Where was Odai?

People told me that some of the injured and martyrs were transferred to Al-Aqsa Martyrs Hospital in Deir al-Balah. I hurried there, still hoping Odai was alive, but couldn't find him. I shouted his name in hospital courtyards and departments, but received no answer. A doctor directed me to the martyrs' tent, and I went immediately.

Joining me in the search for Odai were my son Mohammed, brothers Jihad and Ahmed, and a neighbor. We searched among the many martyrs and found Odai's body. I couldn't believe I had lost him. I hugged him, held his face and body. Shrapnel had injured him behind his ear, chin, and gouged out his right eye. Odai was martyred while working to provide food for us.

With ambulances busy transporting martyrs and those injured, we couldn't find one to take Odai's body to the cemetery. We placed him in a car. I held him, kissed his face throughout the journey. We quickly reached home. I wished the journey could be longer to hold my son.

Family, friends, and neighbors bid farewell to Odai. We prayed for him at the cemetery, where I buried him next to the Great Nuseirat Mosque. It was the worst moment of my life. These are the worst days of my life. I lost my life with Odai's martyrdom.

Two days before his martyrdom, Odai told me he wished to be a martyr defending Palestine. He shared this wish with friends at work, Qusay Yassin and Mohammed Al-Houm, asking if God would forgive them if they were martyred by a rocket. Moments later, a rocket fell, martyring Odai. Mohammed Al-Houm sustained minor injuries, but Qusay Yassin suffered a skull fracture and remains in intensive care.

Since separating from my husband, I have supported my four children alone, striving to provide for them. My dreams were to give them a decent life, but the war shattered all of my plans. I tried opening a small stall in a shelter, but lacked the capital.

My martyr son Odai dreamed of excelling in high school, attending university, and securing a job to provide a good life for us. But the occupation forces killed him, ending his dream, leaving our hearts with enduring pain.

Odai excelled in elementary and preparatory school, but his grades dipped after the separation from my husband. Despite the added expenses, I enrolled him in private lessons in Arabic, math, and English to secure a better future for him. But he earned martyrdom in this war, standing firm on Palestinian land.

I LOST MY SON, MY SUPPORT IN THIS LIFE | 15

Everyone who knew Odai mourns him. His math teacher, Feras Eid, expressed love for Odai, a polite, respectful, hardworking student. Odai dreamed of a better future, lifting us from hardship. His teacher wept for Odai, urging me to care for my other children, who are continuing Odai's journey.

When Israeli forces invaded many central Gaza Strip camps, including Nuseirat camp in January 2024, I fled with my children to tents in Rafah in the southern Gaza Strip. My apartment had sheltered displaced relatives whose homes were bombed. Suddenly, the war had displaced us.

We endured severe suffering in Rafah's tents for a month. The nights cold, the days hot, and rainwater caused hardship. Food, water, and clothes were scarce. After a month, we returned home when the occupation withdrew – a month of suffering.

Before his martyrdom, I hid Odai's schoolbooks from visiting displaced families, unsure if he would return to school. Six months after his martyrdom, I still set a place for him at meals. His body is gone, but his spirit remains with us.

Odai cared for his siblings like a father, affectionate, sharing his allowance, buying them a lot. He dreamed of a better life for us. Now, I dream of continuing Odai's journey, providing my children with a good life, an education, a home, and a stable job. I hope war ends soon. Eight months of continuous killing exhausts us. ♦

Israel Killed Ten Members of My Family in One Airstrike

Rehab Musa Aljamal

❝ Like all people worldwide, we desire security and safety. The occupation must be held accountable for its crimes against our people, especially the massacre of my family, which claimed the lives of ten civilians. ❞

My name is Rehab Musa Aljamal, I am 54 years old from the village of Aqir, which was occupied in 1948. I live with my brothers, their children, and grandchildren in Nuseirat camp in the middle of the Gaza Strip. I was born and spent my childhood, youth, and the rest of my life in this camp.

Our house is located on the main street of the camp, known

to all its residents. It is one of the oldest concrete houses in Gaza, built by my late father over 40 years ago. The house is spacious, exceeding 400 square meters on each floor, and it accommodates six families. Below the house, there are six commercial shops that we rented out. I lived with my brothers and their families until the war began, during which I lost ten members of my family. Today, I am displaced, having lost my house and my eldest brother in an Israeli airstrike on our home.

Since the early days of the Israeli war on the Gaza Strip, which began on October 7, 2023, many of our relatives have sought refuge in our house. My niece Hissab and her four children, my sister Marwa and her three children, my niece Suad and her three children, and my nephew Bayan with his child sought refuge in our house. Before the airstrike, I was in the house along with my eldest brother Azmi's family (four members), my brother Hussam's family (four members), my brother Shahab's family (two members), my brother Emad's family (six members), and my nephew Musa's family (five members). There were 37 people in our house, mostly children and women, seeking safety amid Nuseirat camp's market and nearby UNRWA schools.

On Sunday, October 15, 2023, while arranging my apartment, my sister called to inform me of intensified bombing in Khan Younis city and their evacuation to our house. I prepared for their arrival, but suddenly, amid loud explosions and intense bombing, I was thrown to the ground, covered in blood, sand, and black smoke. Confused and in severe pain, I discovered my severed finger on the ground. In the chaos, my relatives and neighbors found me and rushed me to the hospital for treatment.

During the bombing, my nephew Musa's wife, Ayat Hassan Shaqfa, 35 years old, sustained injuries resulting in the amputation of her left foot, major fractures in her hand requiring surgery and a plate insertion, and severe burns across her body. Her son Azmi, ten years old, suffered burns and fractures, also needing a foot device unavailable in Gaza. Ayat endured hospitalization for a month and a half, only to later learn about the deaths of her uncle Azmi, his wife Hanan, her daughter Nada, and her son Mustafa, with her son Azmi seriously injured in the same hospital.

Ayat, burdened by grief for her children and her husband's family, and the loss of her home, succumbed to her injuries on December 11, 2023, and was buried in Rafah city's family cemetery due to ongoing war conditions preventing burial alongside her children.

My niece Ola sought refuge in our house with her children on the war's first day, only to be killed when our house was bombed a week later. Ola left behind four orphans: Yazan Mahmoud Al-Saedi, ten years old; Zayn, eight years old; Muhammad, five years old; and Sham, three years old. Ola had been married to Mahmoud Al-Saedi for 11 years, residing in Khan Younis city near the European Hospital. Despite completing university with a diploma in medical secretarial work, Ola struggled to find employment in Gaza.

My niece Suad also left behind two orphaned children after her death, including her daughter Janna. Her sons, Omar (ten years old) and Kareem (two years old), survived multiple bombings. Unfortunately, Kareem was killed in an airstrike on his uncle's wife's house. Omar survived with injuries, enduring the harsh conditions of war.

Since my injury over seven months ago, I have been unable to undergo surgery due to the destruction of most hospitals and health centers in Gaza. The few operating facilities function under severe emergency conditions, postponing my necessary surgery. One finger was immediately amputated during the bombing, and I also suffered two fractures and deformities in my hand. Despite current resource constraints, I hope for a successful surgery to save my hand and prevent further loss.

I have endured months of sorrow, pain, and displacement. Following the Israeli invasion of Nuseirat refugee camp in January 2024, I fled with my brother to Rafah city, seeking refuge at my niece Duaa's house for 37 days amid cramped conditions. Currently, I reside in a small rented apartment with my brothers, each occupying separate rooms while I sleep in the living room with their children.

Our house, with its six commercial shops, was a hub for traders offering clothes, shoes, mobile phones, communications, and flowers. Sadly, all the shops were destroyed during the bombing, causing substantial harm to workers dependent on them.

Like all people worldwide, we desire security and safety. The occupation must be held accountable for its crimes against our people, especially the massacre of my family, which claimed the lives of ten civilians. Our household included civilians – men, women, and children. My brother Azmi, beloved in Nuseirat, served as a nurse for decades in the Palestinian Ministry of Health. My brother Imad manages a medical center, while Shahab's wife teaches in UNRWA schools. My brothers and their children work in trade, without affiliation to any political party. This unjustified crime demands accountability.

I pray for an end to this war, the opportunity to rebuild our home, and reunion with my surviving brothers and their children. May our lives soon return to the peace and security we once knew, despite the painful losses we continue to endure. ◆

The Occupation Killed My Grandchildren and Dispersed My Family

Yusra Salem Abu Awad

> **❝** Where is the United Nations? Where are the world's nations? Where are those who stand with us? I raise my voice with all Palestinians. My scattered children, I hope to meet them safely soon. **❞**

SINCE the beginning of the war, my children and I have been scattered across Gaza. I live in a displacement tent in Deir al-Balah, while my children are in tents scattered across Shati camp in Gaza City, Jabalia camp in northern Gaza, and Maghazi camp in central Gaza. The occupation took the lives of three of my grandchildren who fled to Shati camp, denying me the chance to bid them farewell. They were buried in mass graves in Gaza City. My name is Yusra Salem Abu Awad, and I am 63 years old.

The loss of my grandchildren was heartbreaking, but the greatest sorrow inflicted by the occupation is being deprived of saying my final goodbyes. The occupation divides Gaza into the north and south, separating my children and grandchildren in the north from me, my son, and some of my other grandchildren in Deir al-Balah. My family is scattered, and my only dream now is to reunite with my children around one table after the war ends.

Initially, I stayed in my house in Gaza City for a week. When, in the early days of the war, the occupation bombed our residential area, causing extensive damage, I fled. First, I sought refuge in the Nasr neighborhood, then I moved to the Sweidi area of Nasr as the bombing intensified.

For the first month of the war, all 18 of us lived together, moving from place to place in search of safety. As the bombing closed in, my family separated and scattered. Some went to Shati camp with their families, others to the north, some joined me in Deir al-Balah, and the rest fled to Maghazi camp. Our family was dispersed.

Our journey of suffering began with a month of displacement in Sweidi, enduring shelling. We sought refuge at my brother's house in Khan Younis, but the bombing followed us there. We then stayed with my niece in Khan Younis, but again, the bombing forced us to flee to the Mawasi area. After the occupation invaded Khan Younis, intense bombing compelled us to return to displacement tents in Deir al-Balah.

I am accustomed to having my children around me, living together in a multi-floor house. We used to gather every Friday for lunch. But in this war, we are separated. I cannot sleep, constantly thinking of them and yearning for our reunion. The war has dragged on for over seven months, and I miss my children dearly. I long to have my family together again.

My son remains with his family in Shati camp, seeking refuge in UNRWA schools like Abu Assi School. They endured the occupation's invasion of Gaza City and Shati camp, living in constant fear and facing prolonged periods of hunger, but they survived.

Tragically, my grandchildren were killed by an Israeli airstrike targeting the vicinity of the school sheltering them. Three of my grandchildren perished in the airstrike, innocent victims of injustice, oppression, pain, and hunger during this war. Their father tried to protect them, fleeing from the bombing, but the airstrikes found them at the UNRWA school and took their lives.

What crime did these children commit for the occupation to kill them? *Is their only fault being Palestinian?* The occupation took the lives of my second-grade grandson, first-grade grandson, and one-year-old granddaughter. Why were they deprived of their lives, leaving us to mourn their loss? *Is their only fault being Palestinian?* The occupation committed these atrocities and must be held accountable.

The crimes inflicted upon us since the war's beginning are immense. For nearly eight months, the occupation has not ceased its crimes, escalating daily in killing and destroying Gaza. This is not a solution. These crimes must stop. The destruction of Gaza in this war must cease. The world must stand for justice for the Palestinian people.

We call upon Arab countries, international organizations, non-governmental organizations, and all legal bodies to support the oppressed Palestinian people. Why must we endure such injustice? *Is our only fault being Palestinian?* What we suffer in this war exceeds what any human can bear. It must stop immediately.

We once lived in dignified homes, beautiful concrete structures built over years at great expense to shelter our children. Now, we live in tents lacking basic human necessities.

Life in the tents we've inhabited for over six months is intolerable. There is no water or electricity. There are no beds or bathrooms. Insects torment us. This is not a liveable condition. All we experience is a disgrace that will haunt the occupation and the international community for their complicity in this accursed war.

Israel fights us while occupying our land, and we defend our land. By Allah, my martyred grandchildren were temporarily buried in shelters. We await the war's end to bury them properly. This is not a solution. We demand an immediate solution. We demand to return to our homes and land in Gaza.

We are a people who desire peace and yearn to live in peace. We have suffered since our displacement in 1948, enduring bombing and death throughout the occupation's existence. We do not deserve this treatment. We seek peace and demand the release of our prisoners, just as the occupation demands the release of its prisoners.

I appeal to all nations to intervene and find a solution for us. I appeal to Arab and Islamic nations to stand with us, ending the genocide we face. We do not seek supplies or flour. We seek to live with peace, security, and freedom. This is our plea to the United Nations and all who stand with the Palestinian people.

We have no solutions in our hands. This Nakba is greater than that of 1948, the third catastrophe for the Palestinian people. The occupation's actions in this war shame us all. Where is the United Nations? Where are the world's nations? Where are those who stand with us? I raise my voice with all Palestinians. My scattered children, I hope to meet them safely soon.

I am in Deir al-Balah, my son in the north of Gaza, my other son in Shati camp, and another in Maghazi camp. Gaza is small, yet we have not seen each other since the war began. We have not reunited. I know nothing of my sons. My life's dream is to reunite with them in one home before my death, to live in peace and security, and to secure a safe future for our children, ensuring this war is Gaza's last. It is time for Gaza's people to live in peace and for the Israeli occupation to cease its killings. ♦

I Lost My Beautiful Father at 12 Years Old

Youssef Qawash

> During this war, my father lost his job. He spent more time with us, trying to reassure us that the bombing was far from our home. We felt safe in his presence, cherishing every moment with him. Little did we know that we were bidding him farewell during those last days we spent together with our beloved father.

SINCE the onset of the Israeli war on the Gaza Strip in October 2023, my family and I have lived in constant fear due to the relentless Israeli bombardments. The occupation targeted a house neighboring ours, causing extensive damage to our home. We sought refuge at our grandmother's house in Rafah, while my father remained in Nuseirat camp in central Gaza. Tragically, a few days after our departure to Rafah, our house was bombed by the occupation, resulting in the deaths of my father, my uncle, and dozens of our neighbors. The loss of our father has left us to face the war without his support.

My name is Youssef Qawash, and I am 12 years old. I live with my mother, Hanan, who teaches religious education at a Palestinian government school. I have four brothers: Bilal, 14 years old; Suwar, ten years old; Anwar, six years old; and my youngest brother Ahmed, four years old. Our father, Ayman, provided for our family. Our lives were beautiful together, but they have now become miserable after the loss of our father and the destruction of our home.

My father meant everything to us. He worked as a civil engineer, managing his own engineering office located on the first floor of our house. Before the war, due to work commitments, we didn't see much of him during the week. However, he always made sure to organize a weekly outing for us. We would go to Gaza City, visit a small amusement park, dine together at a restaurant, and enjoy desserts before returning home joyfully. Our father's presence was our greatest joy.

During this war, my father lost his job. He spent more time with us, trying to reassure us that the bombing was far from our home. We felt safe in his presence, cherishing every moment with him. Little did we know that we were bidding him farewell during those last days we spent together with our beloved father.

In early January 2024, occupation forces entered the camps in central Gaza, including Nuseirat where we lived. They ordered all residents to evacuate. We fled once again to our grandmother's house in Rafah, but our father chose to stay behind in our house. Tearfully, we said goodbye to him and left for Rafah. It would be the last time we saw our father.

A few days later, while we were in Rafah, the occupation bombed the residential area where we had lived, completely destroying two houses, including ours. My father, Ayman Anwar Qawash, 37, was martyred in the bombing, along with my uncle Hussam, a nurse at Al-Shifa Hospital, and more than 18 neighbors from the Al-Shabrawi family, most of them children.

We received news of the bombing while in Rafah. My uncles, Dr. Mohammed and Abdul Latif, went to Al-Aqsa Martyrs Hospital to search for my father and uncle Hussam. They found my uncle Hussam martyred at the hospital, but my father was not among the identified bodies. Many martyrs arrived at the hospital unidentifiable due to their condition and were buried in a mass grave. To this day, we do not know if my father was among them or if he remains buried under the rubble of our home. The lack of equipment has prevented us from retrieving his body.

Losing our father and uncle in the bombing was a devastating blow. We also lost our home, where my grandfather and uncles lived. Each uncle had their own apartment, and there was a large apartment for my grandfather. My father had recently built a floor for us and furnished it completely before he was martyred. Now, we have lost our provider and our home. We are homeless.

Like all children in the world, it is my right to live in dignity, security, and peace. Like all children who have lost a parent, it is my right to visit my father's grave and know where he is buried. For the past four months, I have searched every cemetery in Al-Qassam in the middle of Nuseirat camp, southern Nuseirat, and Al-Shubani west of the camp. My uncles have searched in Deir al-Balah and Maghazi, but no one knows where my father is buried. This uncertainty is a pain beyond what we can bear.

Our ground-floor house included two dental clinics: one for my grandfather, Dr. Anwar, a renowned dentist, and one for my uncle, Dr. Mohammed, who worked alongside two nurses. Both clinics were destroyed by the occupation, leaving the staff without jobs and patients without care. Despite the war, my uncle Mohammed continued to treat patients.

The occupation also destroyed my father's private engineering office, where he had designed housing plans for many families. We lost the income that supported our livelihood. The occupation has taken everything from us in this war.

Previously, we had food, water, and all our needs met thanks to our father. My brothers and I excelled in our studies. Now, we struggle to find food, often having only one or two meals a day. Water is scarce, and there is no education available, as schools, mostly spared from Israeli bombing, have become shelters for displaced people. We have lost an entire academic year due to the war.

At the beginning of September 2023, we started a new school year. I began sixth grade at UNRWA schools with my siblings. Just one month later, the war began, halting life in Gaza. Schools became shelters for thousands of displaced people, and classrooms turned into sleeping quarters. Many of my classmates and teachers were martyred, and Israeli airstrikes destroyed dozens of schools and universities across Gaza, causing widespread destruction.

We were supposed to sit for semester exams in January 2024 and end-of-year exams in June 2024. However, with the war now in its eighth month, and only a month left in the academic year, all students in Gaza have lost this school year and a year of their lives amid ongoing war and destruction caused by the occupation.

Every child in the world has the right to learn in a safe environment, to live with loved ones, and to live without occupation. The occupation has committed countless atrocities against us, disregarding international humanitarian law. The children of Gaza have grown up far too quickly, enduring unimaginable hardships and suffering in this war.

No compensation in life can replace the loss of our father. He was everything to us, and losing him has shattered our lives. The occupation has left me and my younger siblings without a father, without a home, and without means to support ourselves. We pray for an end to this war, and for the occupation to be held accountable for its crimes against Palestinians in Gaza during more than seven months of intense warfare. ♦

Three Days Without Food or Water

Fatima Ahmed Abu Bakra

❝ I built a modest house and have been living in it for 40 years. My family has been in danger all our lives because of our proximity to the border, but I consider this place my life and I feel a strong connection to it. ❞

I LIVE with my deaf children in the eastern part of Bureij refugee camp, in the Gaza Strip. We left our house under heavy shelling in mid-October 2023, on the third day of the Israeli war. We fled to the UNRWA schools in Bureij camp, then we moved to Khan Younis city, and finally returned to a tent at the entrance of Bureij. We lived there for three days without food or water. These were the toughest days I have experienced in my 80 years of life. My name is Fatima Ahmed Abu Bakra.

I am a Palestinian woman, 80 years old, born before the Nakba in 1948. I was four years old when Palestine was occupied. I experienced the suffering of displacement after the Nakba, and now I am enduring the unprecedented and ferocious war on the Gaza Strip, ongoing for more than seven months. I witnessed the occupation of Palestine, and today I witness hundreds of massacres committed by the occupation against more than 2.3 million Palestinians living in the Gaza Strip.

I got married when I was 16 years old and gave birth to five sons: Ayman, Salmaan, Mohammed, Radwan, and Ahmed, and five daughters: Iman, Hanan, Safaa, Hanaa, and Wafa. Four of my sons are deaf and mute. I separated from my husband 40 years ago.

I live with my deaf children and 27 grandchildren in my house in the eastern part of Bureij camp, on the eastern border separating us from our occupied lands. I built a modest house and have been living in it for 40 years. My family has been in danger all our lives because of our proximity to the border, but I consider this place my life and I feel a strong connection to it.

In 2006, the occupation forces waged a war for several days after Palestinian fighters captured the Israeli soldier Gilad Shalit. During this conflict, my deaf son Ahmed was wandering behind our house. He left without hearing the sound of gunfire, heading to Maghazi camp. The occupation forces shot him three times in the chest, and he was martyred instantly. Also, my sons' half-brother from their father, named Fadi, was martyred, and the occupation arrested their half-brother from their father, named Muntasir.

I've struggled a lot in my life, and I managed to get my son Mohammed, the only one of my sons who is not deaf, into university. He obtained a bachelor's degree in Arabic language, but could not find a job in the Gaza Strip due to the continued Israeli siege in place since 2006. He used to work as a taxi driver, but during the war he lost his job, and then there was no one to provide for us.

After working hard, I managed to marry off all of my sons and now have grandchildren. My son Mohammed has eight children: Maaz, 13 years old; Ahmed, 12 years old; Muawiyah, seven years old; Mohammed, four months old (born during the war); Amira, 15 years old; Fatima, 13 years old; Khadijah, five years old; and Sara, four years old. My son Ayman has four children: Adnan, seven years old; Halima, four years old; Amina, three years old; and Ghalia, two years old. My son Salmaan had two daughters. My daughter Hanan had four sons and two daughters. My daughter Iman had three sons and one daughter. My daughter Hanaa had a son and two daughters. My son Ahmed was martyred before getting married. I have my daughter Safaa, 40 years old, who lives with me and never married.

On the third day of the Israeli occupation's war on the Gaza Strip, after intense Israeli shelling of the eastern areas of Bureij camp, my children, grandchildren, and I, numbering over 20, fled. We only managed to save our lives; we couldn't take anything from the house, just the clothes on our backs.

The shelling was severe, and I hugged my children and grandchildren. We ran under the bombardment together. I was hit by shrapnel in my head and foot, and I still suffer from my injuries to this day. We reached Abu Halou's schools in Bureij camp, running more than two kilometers [1.2 miles] under the shelling, thinking we had reached a safe place in the UNRWA school.

We stayed in the schools set up as shelters in Bureij camp for two months. After the occupation forces raided the camps of the central governorate of the Gaza Strip, we fled to Khan Younis city. We lived there for two weeks in the open, unable to find a tent to live in. We endured the heavy rain and cold without shelter.

My son Mohammed's wife gave birth to her son Mohammed while we were living in the displacement tents in Rafah city. Those were very difficult days. The newborn lived with us in the open. We stayed in Khan Younis for about three weeks, and after the occupation withdrew from the camps of Bureij, Maghazi, and Nuseirat, we returned to Bureij camp.

We couldn't return to our home in the eastern part of Bureij camp because the occupation vehicles were close to our house. We learned from our neighbors that the occupation had completely destroyed our house. I was forced to live with my children in a small shack without a door, in a house under construction at the western entrance of Bureij camp.

We were among the first displaced people to return to Bureij camp. We found only a few residents. The shelling was intense everywhere. We spent three days without food or water. We had no money, and there were no markets, no sellers, and no institutions in Bureij camp from which to get food. We found nothing to eat.

The children cried a lot. We lived in this cramped place, unsuitable for living, with more than 20 other displaced people, mostly children and women. I used to go out with my children searching for food and water, but we couldn't find any. Fear filled all our hearts, but we managed to stay alive. Everyone survived by drinking a little water. We got a little food on the fourth day after our return from Khan Younis.

Since the early days of the war on Gaza, I have known nothing about my deaf son Salmaan, who lives in Rafah city near his wife's family home. I tried to reach him, to contact him, and to check on him and his children, but I couldn't. I searched a lot for him, but I haven't heard any news about him.

I suffer from chronic hypertension and severe pain in my foot. I've been suffering from my head and foot injuries since the early days of the war. I have become forgetful due to the injury, but my heart is attached to my sons and my house in the eastern part of Bureij camp. I have lived in this house for over 40 years. I've lived my youth and old age in it. I bid farewell to my son as a martyr there and watched my grandchildren play in it. My house means everything to us.

My dream is to see my son Salmaan again, to be able to meet him again. I hope he is safe and has not been hit by the occupation's rockets and shells. I wish to see him, to embrace him and my grandchildren soon. I dream of being able to rebuild my house anew, to keep my children around me until the last day of my life.

I lost my son Ahmed as a martyr in 2006. In this newest war, I have been injured in my head and foot. The occupation destroyed my house, and it separated me from my son Salmaan. We've lived more than seven months in extremely difficult conditions. We are still homeless, but we love this land, and we are ready to live in a tent on top of our destroyed houses. We will never leave Gaza. This is our land, and the occupation must leave. The occupation must be tried for all its crimes against us, and for all the suffering we have endured since the first day of the war. We are currently living as displaced people on the little aid we receive from relief organizations. Our demand is not just food and water – our demand is the liberation of our homeland and our return to our homes destroyed by the occupation during this oppressive war.

My Husband Was Martyred and There Is No Body: My Story of Pain Caused by the Israeli Occupation

Somia Issa Mustafa Saleh

> ❝ I am currently the mother and father to my children. My family and my husband's family are in Gaza City. I live alone with my children; I always accompany them. We go to the bathroom together, and we go to receive the small food basket every ten days together. I'm afraid to go down to the schoolyard, thinking I may be killed by the occupying forces' shelling. ❞

THE day before the war, my family and I celebrated my sister's wedding. The celebrations lasted for several days leading up to the wedding day, which was Friday, October 6, 2023. After the wedding, I stayed at my family's home with my children. The war began while I was there, and I still haven't returned to my home, which has now been destroyed by the occupation. My husband was killed by an Israeli sniper while searching for water.

My name is Somia Issa Mustafa Saleh, 32 years old, from Jabalia refugee camp in the northern Gaza Strip. I got married five years ago to Abdullah Saleh, and we lived our lives in a humble home in Jabalia camp. We had two children, Ahmed Saleh, four years old, and Adi Saleh, two years old. We lived happily until October 7, 2023.

I couldn't return to my home after the wedding due to the severe Israeli bombardment on Jabalia camp, beginning the first day of the war. I stayed with my husband and children at my parents' house in Jabalia camp for 20 days. Due to the intense and violent shelling, which targeted neighboring houses, we decided to leave.

We fled to Asmaa School in the Shati camp west of Gaza City. We walked on foot for more than 13 kilometers [8.1 miles] and lived in the school for two weeks. The Israeli occupation forces issued warning leaflets, demanding that we evacuate the school, so we evacuated again. This time, I went with my husband and children to Khan Younis city, south of Gaza Valley. It was considered one of the safe areas, as designated by the occupation force.

We stayed in one of the UNRWA shelters in Khan Younis city for two months. After the first ceasefire ended, the war resumed more intensely, and the Israeli operation began in Khan Younis city. The occupation planes dropped leaflets demanding that we leave the city. The shelling was severe and intense. Some of us managed to leave, but many couldn't. My husband, my children, and I were among those who couldn't leave the school. I was afraid for my children because of the severity of the violent shelling carried out by the occupation forces on the city.

On January 29, 2024, the water supply to the school was completely cut off. Our displaced neighbors in the school asked my husband to go up to the roof to check the water because the children and everyone trapped inside the school were suffering from severe thirst.

My husband went up to the school roof, and several hours passed without him coming down. It was already eleven o'clock at night when I climbed up to the school roof to search for my husband Abdullah, but I couldn't find him. I thought he had come down from the roof without me seeing him, so I left the school and went to the displacement tents west of the city to search for him, but I couldn't find him.

I searched for my husband until one of the other displaced people informed me that he had been martyred by a gunshot from the Israeli tanks on the school roof. I decided to return to the school to confirm the news. As I climbed up to the school roof, the Israeli artillery started shelling the school and its surroundings heavily. I was shocked by the scene I saw: my husband lying on the school roof amid a large pool of blood, lifeless, shot by an Israeli sniper.

I couldn't control myself from the shock of the scene. I crawled toward the place where my husband was, amid heavy gunfire, tied his leg, and tried to pull him down, but I couldn't. I asked for help from the other displaced people, but due to the intensity of the Israeli shelling, we couldn't get him down. So I left him on the school roof, and we all left the school for the displacement tents.

The journey out of the school was harsh and extremely dangerous. Gunfire was continuous and shelling was everywhere. We left amid destruction, Israeli artillery fire, and airstrikes, but I had to leave to protect my children's lives. I lost my husband as a martyr, and I didn't want to lose my children to the Israeli bombardment.

I spent three days in the tents, thinking about my husband. My tragedy was great; my husband was martyred, leaving me with two children. I loved my husband, and I wanted to bury him in the cemetery. I didn't want his body to remain on the school roof, to be eaten by stray dogs. I slept with my children in the tents for three days without light, food, or water.

After several days, I contacted the UNRWA operations and asked for help in bringing down my husband from the school roof and burying him. But, due to the intense shelling, they couldn't help me. So I went back to search for my husband's body on the school roof, bringing my children with me. We walked for more than two hours, exposed to direct gunfire, and I managed to reach the school with difficulty.

I hurriedly climbed up to the school roof to bring my husband down, but I couldn't find his body. I don't know who brought him down from the roof, and I don't know where he was buried. I still don't know anything. I don't know anything about the whereabouts of my husband's burial place. Did other displaced people bury him in a cemetery inside the school? Did the occupation forces throw his body into a mass grave, as they have often done in this painful war?

I returned to the displacement tent in a bad mental state, as my husband, my love, and my life companion was martyred. I still don't know where he's buried. I lived alone with my children for about two weeks, with nothing. My family and my husband's family remained in Gaza City and did not leave like we did. I lost my phone during that period and lost all contact with my family.

For two weeks, my children and I relied on aid from our displaced neighbors. I managed to get a tent for myself and my children. After the Israeli shelling intensified, I moved to the Nuseirat camp in the middle of the Gaza Strip. I lived for a month and a half in the house of one of my relatives. After a neighboring house was shelled, I moved to a school run by UNRWA to shelter the displaced in the Nuseirat camp, where I've been living with my children for over a month.

Since the beginning of the war, my children and I have faced harsh living conditions, but after my husband's martyrdom, our suffering increased. We lost our support. We lost our strength and energy and our passion for life after his death. It is very difficult to provide food and water for my family. We have no source of income to live on. We have no clothes besides the ones we wear.

I had managed to get some more clothes after arriving at a school-turned-shelter in the Nuseirat camp, but the occupying forces shelled the school, and the clothes were completely burned. Our children don't have shoes to wear; they walk and wander barefoot in the school. I suffer a lot in my life at the school, as I am a displaced person in a classroom with about ten families and their children. I have one mattress for myself and my children; the classroom is on the third floor, and the school's public bathrooms are on the first floor, with no water in the bathrooms. The school has been shelled three times.

I am currently the mother and father to my children. My family and my husband's family are in Gaza City. I live alone with my children; I always accompany them. We go to the bathroom together, and we go to receive the small food basket every ten days together. I'm afraid to go down to the schoolyard, thinking I may be killed by the occupying forces' shelling. Dozens of displaced people have been killed or injured by the repeated shelling of the school.

When my husband was martyred, it left me with the great responsibility of raising our children. I lost my home in the violent shelling by the occupying forces on the Jabalia camp, and I lost my husband in this war. I live on aid with my children. I hope the war will end soon. I hope to find my husband's burial place. I hope my destroyed home in the Jabalia camp will be rebuilt. I dream of being able to secure a dignified future for my children; they are my husband's trust to me, and they are all I have left in this life. ♦

The Occupation Arrested My Sick Husband and We Live in Constant Suffering

Shaymaa Al-Eisswei

❝ We have moved from one tent camp to another, carrying the same tent with us. This tent has witnessed all our suffering since the beginning of the war. It does not protect us from the winter cold, rain, or the high temperatures. We dream of returning to our homes. ❞

After undergoing thorough inspections at checkpoints set up by the occupation at the entrance of the city, we managed to leave and fled to displacement tents in Deir al-Balah.

I was a Palestinian woman living in the city of Hamad with my family. We were happy to receive an apartment from the Ministry of Social Development, affiliated with the Palestinian government in the Gaza Strip. We lived in the apartment for several years, and our life was beautiful in our new home. However, the occupation destroyed our joy and our home.

Israeli occupation forces intensified their fierce bombardment on Khan Younis city after a ceasefire that had lasted for one week ended in late November 2023. Before the ceasefire, we endured severe Israeli bombardment that resulted in many casualties. The situation worsened when the occupation forces invaded the city in mid-December 2023, leaving the city in indescribable devastation.

The Israeli occupation forces invaded Khan Younis twice. During the first invasion, they bombed buildings and apartments in Hamad, but did not enter and destroy the city as they did during the second invasion, which left the city devastated.

After living in tents for many days, and after the first withdrawal of the occupation from Khan Younis, my husband, who suffers from heart disease, went to check on our house in Hamad. He found it destroyed, but the building had not completely collapsed. The walls were demolished, and the furniture was ruined.

Despite his heart condition and chronic diseases requiring daily medication, my husband insisted on returning to our house. He went ahead of us, cleaned the destroyed house, and put up makeshift zinc walls around our apartment. We lived there for one week before the occupation invaded the city again. It was a very difficult week under bombardment. We spent two days trying to leave through occupation checkpoints, and on our third attempt, the occupation arrested my husband while we were leaving the city. My children and I then returned to Deir al-Balah and resumed living in tents, as the occupation had destroyed our apartment.

My husband's name is Jamal Bajes Al-Eisswei. He is an elderly man who worked in electrical installations, a job that completely stopped at the beginning of the war. We depended on him for everything.

He was arrested by the occupation forces on February 3, 2024, and held for two months. During his absence, we suffered greatly. The occupation forces fired at us while we were trying to leave Hamad, forcing us to return multiple times. We finally succeeded on the third day, but my husband was arrested in the process.

For two months, we had no information about my husband's whereabouts. We contacted the Red Cross, but received no news. Thankfully, he was released after 60 days, though his shoulder and chest were injured from the torture he endured in detention. Now, he is unable to work, and we cannot bear life in the tents any longer.

Living in tents for over four months has been extremely difficult. The tents are unbearably hot, especially with the rising temperatures. My children and grandchildren have developed skin diseases and allergies. The infestation of insects in the tents is severe, and there are no pesticides to combat them. Despite cleaning the tent daily, the situation remains dire. There is no proper waste disposal, leading to health problems, foul odors, and more insect infestations.

We have moved from one tent camp to another, carrying the same tent with us. This tent has witnessed all our suffering since the beginning of the war. It does not protect us from the winter cold, rain, or the high temperatures. We dream of returning to our homes.

My son, Mohammed Al-Eisswei, got married in August 2023, about two months before the war. He lived in an apartment adjacent to ours, which he had beautifully furnished. He spent large sums of money preparing his apartment, but the war forced him to move into tents with us. The occupation deprived him of enjoying his new life. When he went to inspect his apartment after the occupation forces withdrew, he found it completely destroyed, losing years of hard work and effort.

My son's wife found out she was pregnant a month after their wedding. She suffered through more than seven months of the war and gave birth to my first grandchild, Jamal, a month ago. We struggle to provide milk and diapers for him. The baby suffers from the heat and insect bites in the tents. I hope the war ends and God grants my grandson a better life than ours.

Before the war, after years of living in rented houses, we had finally received, with great difficulty, a residential apartment in Hamad city. We were very happy, but the occupation did not allow us to enjoy it. The war broke out in October 2023, forcing us to flee to the Nuseirat camp and then to Deir al-Balah. We spent the winter in tents, enduring severe cold. Now, we face the unbearable heat.

For nearly eight months, we have lived in tragedy, losing many relatives as martyrs. The occupation bombed our homes, leaving us homeless and living in tents. We receive a small food basket weekly, barely enough for one meal a day. Our children are always hungry.

No one addresses our suffering or intervenes to stop the war and the occupation's crimes. Tens of thousands of martyrs and wounded have fallen among us, and most of the population in Gaza lives in tents. May God have mercy on all the martyrs and heal all the wounded. We hope to return to our homes soon.

But I have no home now. My son has no home. The occupation greatly destroyed Hamad city. After the occupation withdrew, we found the city devastated, not as we left it. I hope my husband recovers from his injuries and the war ends so we can live a safe life.

We are tired of this war. Our children are exhausted, and we don't know what to do for them. No one addresses our suffering or works to stop the war. The bombing is everywhere, and we feel our turn is coming. We hope the war stops, so we can return to our lives. We're tired of hearing the bombings, but this is our reality now. May God ease these days for the Palestinian people. Everyone is suffering, and everyone is tired. Praise be to God in all circumstances. Hopefully, the war will end soon, and all the prisoners will be released from the occupation's prisons. ♦

The Occupation Killed My Husband and Left Me with Our Three Children

Shaymaa Al-Durra

❝ Every day, my children ask me about their father. They say, 'Mama, why has Daddy been delayed in returning? Daddy took a long time and hasn't returned yet.' I tell them that their father will return soon, that he went to bring us food, and that he is at work now and will come back with everything we want. ❞

In 2014, I married the young man Muhammad Sami Al-Durra, and we were a small, happy Palestinian family. We had three children and lived very happily for the nine years preceding this war. However, the occupation bombed our house in the early days of the war on Gaza, forcing us to seek refuge in UNRWA schools. Then, the occupation killed my husband, leaving our three children without a father.

Since the first day of the war, my children have been living under difficult psychological conditions. We are displaced people living in an UNRWA school in the Nuseirat camp in the middle of the Gaza Strip. The occupation bombed the residential area in which we lived in the Bureij camp. We survived the bombing, but for six months, we have been living in distress, homeless and displaced.

My husband, Muhammad, worked as a day laborer in the Gaza Strip. Our financial situation was difficult, as is the case for the majority of Gaza's residents, but he did his best to provide for our household's needs and the needs of our children: Hamza, nine years old; Sami, seven years old; and our daughter, Wateen, who is two years old. Muhammad tried to provide for all their needs, but the Israeli war on Gaza was beyond his capabilities and made life for everyone very difficult.

In the first week of the war, the occupation destroyed our house, and we were displaced to a school affiliated with UNRWA in Nuseirat. We now live with eight families in one classroom, with only women and children sleeping inside. My husband, his father, and his brothers slept in the schoolyard. My children wished their father could sleep with us in the same place as we did before the war, but the circumstances prevented this simple request.

After we were displaced to the UNRWA school, my husband worked as a volunteer in the relief efforts and in the securing of the school. He, along with many other young displaced people, stayed up all night guarding the school to protect it from theft. He also volunteered to unload aid in the school stores and distribute it to the displaced families.

Muhammad formed a special relationship with the school administration and the police personnel who helped guard the school. He loved life and was dedicated to providing for all our needs, especially those of our infant daughter, Wateen. I asked him not to leave the school, and to stay with us for fear of bombing, but he insisted on going out to search for work and food for us.

During the fifth month of the war, my husband went out to look for food for us. He wandered around the Nuseirat camp market and visited several aid distribution points. We receive one food basket every two weeks, which is not enough. We live in difficult conditions and have lost a lot of weight. My husband's only concern was to provide food for our son, which made him risk his life to obtain some aid for us.

On the morning of the first Monday of April 2024, my husband went out in a city car belonging to the school security to bring food aid for the hundreds of displaced families at the school. Meters away from the school, Israeli occupation planes bombed the car, killing my husband and several others, including displaced people and policemen. Many more were injured in the attack.

My son Hamza saw his father in a dream, surrounded by people who were hugging him. This dream became a reality a few days later when my husband was transferred from Al-Awda Hospital in the Nuseirat camp to the school serving as a shelter where we live. My son bid farewell to his father, placing a final kiss on his face. Funeral prayers were performed at the school. We were unable to bury him in the Bureij camp cemetery due to nearby occupation forces, so we buried him in the Nuseirat camp cemetery.

The occupation deprived us of living in the Bureij camp, where we were born, grew up, and raised our family. It also deprived my husband of being buried in the camp cemetery. The war has been ongoing for more than seven months, and these have been the most difficult and cruel months of our lives. Gaza has endured many wars and attacks since the Israeli occupation in 1967, but this war is unparalleled in its cruelty, pain, death, injustice, hunger, and destruction.

I was married to a young man I loved deeply, and together we formed a beautiful family. I lived happily with him for more than nine years. Today, I find myself a widow, deprived of my husband, my support, and everything in my life. Muhammad was beautiful in all his qualities, loving everyone and always eager to help.

The occupation deprived my three children of their father. Muhammad left me with a great responsibility – to raise, care for, and support our three orphaned children. He dreamed of seeing his children complete their education and pursue careers that would provide them with a better future. Now, they are without a father and without support. The occupation shed Muhammad's blood and left us to face life's hardships alone.

I was strong during the first five months of the war because my husband, Muhammad, was with me, protecting us and providing for our needs. But now, we have lost this support, the one who cared for us and ensured our happiness. We have lost tenderness, security, happiness – everything. The occupation killed my husband Muhammad and created immense pain in our souls.

Every day, my children ask me about their father. They say, "Mama, why has Daddy been delayed in returning? Daddy took a long time and hasn't returned yet." I tell them that their father will return soon, that he went to bring us food, and that he is at work now and will come back with everything we want.

I don't know what to tell my children. These days, I try not to expose them to more psychological trauma. The trauma they have experienced since the beginning of the war is enough. My eldest son, Hamza, knows that his father was martyred and bid him farewell at the school. But my son Sami, and my infant daughter Wateen, do not know that the occupation killed their father. I am trying to hide this from them until the war ends and stops completely.

Every day, I try to distract my children by playing in the schoolyard and encouraging them to participate in entertainment activities organized by youth teams. They play in the small remaining part of the schoolyard. Dozens of families have set up their tents in the yard, and the children can only play in the small part that remains open. Everything around us reminds us of displacement, war, killing, and the loss of loved ones.

My husband Muhammad dreamed of building or buying an apartment for us, as we lived in rented apartments for many years. But Muhammad passed away, killed by the occupation before this wish could be fulfilled. I hope to complete Muhammad's mission, to provide an apartment for my children, and to educate them so their father will be proud of them in his grave. They are proud to be the children of the martyr Muhammad Sami Al-Durra, who was martyred refusing to emigrate from Gaza, determined to remain on this land to give his children a decent life.

We live in difficult conditions in the displacement centers. We do not always have food or clean water. We suffer from a lack of water. My children have no clothes or shoes, and there is no security or safety in the school. Bombing surrounds us on all sides; the occupation bombed the school we were displaced to twice, and several displaced people were martyred inside. I always stay close to my children, not wanting the bombing to harm them. I want to live the rest of my life with my children and die with them. My youth and dreams are lost, but I will not lose my purpose – to raise my children and protect them from all dangers.

We urgently hope the war on Gaza will stop. Over more than seven months, we have been exposed to all forms of injustice and genocide. The war must stop. We must return to our homes. America and the international community must work sincerely to stop the war and urgently rebuild Gaza. ✦

The Stolen Childhood of Palestinian Children

Saeed Al-Halabi

❝ I am very afraid of the sounds of shelling and gunfire, but we have become accustomed to hearing them in the eighth month of the war. I dream that the war will stop, and people will return to their homes, and we will return to our schools, complete our education, and end all this suffering imposed by the occupation. ❞

Every day, I leave my home in the early morning to work. I head to a school belonging to UNRWA in the Nuseirat refugee camp, which shelters thousands of displaced people. I continue working inside the school until the evening hours. I earn some money, never more than 20 Israeli shekels per day. I give the money to my father, who lost his job during the war, to help my family with household expenses and to provide some food for my 12 siblings. This has been my daily life since the beginning of the Israeli war on Gaza.

I live with my brothers and sisters in a simple house in the Nuseirat camp, in the middle of the Gaza Strip. I have three sisters, and the rest are boys. I am the oldest among my siblings. I study in the seventh preparatory grade, and my academic average is 75%. I have been working for years during summer vacations, holidays, and special occasions to help my father because his salary is not enough to meet the needs of our large family.

My father worked in a sweets factory in Gaza City called Abu Al-Saud Sweets Factory, one of the most famous sweets factories in the Gaza Strip. It is located south of the Al-Shifa Medical Complex, where my father worked for several years. But on the first day of the Israeli occupation's war on the Gaza Strip, my father lost his job.

My father was unable to go to work in the early days of the war due to the intense Israeli bombardment. After the occupation began its ground assault on the Gaza Strip at the end of October 2023, it separated the north of the Gaza Strip from the south. This completely prevented my father from accessing his workplace.

After the occupation invaded Gaza City and reached the Al-Shifa Medical Complex, the occupation warplanes bombed the sweets factory where my father worked, destroying it and depriving my father of his job. The bombing also deprived dozens of my father's colleagues of work, and they all became unemployed. Before the war, there was a 70% unemployment rate among youth in the Gaza Strip.

I've owned trampolines since before the war. I used to rent them out during events and summer vacations. But in the early days of the war, after my father lost his job, I started my simple trampoline business at Al-Jaouni School in the middle of the Nuseirat camp. Al-Jaouni School is affiliated with UNRWA, and is crowded with thousands of displaced people.

I go to the school every day. Children play on the trampolines for a few minutes in exchange for one Israeli shekel. I spend over 12 hours at the school. On many days, I don't even make 5 shekels because the displaced people don't have money. They've lost their jobs, homes, and providers. They rely entirely on aid.

I'm afraid to put the trampolines outside the school's sheltered areas because Israeli bombardment is everywhere. Even the school where I work was bombed twice by the occupation forces. Many displaced people were martyred or wounded there. But God saved me from the bombing both times.

In the first bombing of the school, I was standing at the school's gate, and the occupation bombed the school yard. In the second bombing, I was going to repair the trampoline, and the bombing happened very close to where I usually place the trampoline. But God saved me. I fear that I will be killed or injured and disabled by the occupation's missiles. I see hundreds of wounded and injured every day in shelters.

During the Eid al-Fitr, several youth groups organized a "Holiday Joy" event for displaced children at the school. I joined them in entertaining the children and opened the trampoline game for them to play for free. I was happy to bring joy to the faces of displaced children. While I need money to help my family, I was extremely happy with this beautiful humanitarian work.

Trampolines constantly need repairs. They have numerous iron assemblies and fabric pieces for children to jump on. The iron gets broken, and the fabric tears. Before this war, I used to repair them for a small amount, but now, repairing them has become very costly.

I used to weld several iron pieces for ten Israeli shekels before the war, but during the war, welding one piece costs 20 shekels. I also need to sew the fabric at the tailor's shop, but there has been no electricity in Gaza since the first day of the war. This lack has forced me to learn hand sewing to sew them myself, but the quality is different from what a sewing machine would provide.

When the occupation forces invaded the central camps of the Gaza Strip at the beginning of January 2024, we fled to the city of

Deir al-Balah to escape the Israeli shelling. I left the trampolines at the school and left with my family in search of safety. We stayed in tents for over three weeks, then returned to our home, which was heavily damaged by the Israeli shelling that hit large areas across the camp.

My cousin, Akram Saeed Al-Halabi, 18 years old, fled the Israeli missiles. While walking on Salah al-Din Street heading to Rafah, the occupation aircraft bombed him, and he was martyred instantly. He was buried without us being able to bid him farewell. After the occupation forces withdrew, we dug up his grave to confirm his identity. After confirming, we reburied him away from our homes in Khan Younis near the tents of the displaced people.

The occupation bulldozers destroyed my uncles' houses during the incursion into Bureij camp. The occupation also bombed and destroyed my uncle's house on Salah al-Din Street. Our house was significantly damaged, like all the houses in Gaza. We walk daily among the rubble, living amid the ruins, bidding farewell to our loved ones and relatives every day. We have lost a lot in this war.

I continue to work while studying because I dream of completing my university education, getting a job in the future to help my family with our expenses, and securing my family's and my future. I now feel tired and exhausted, and I hope to rest from this fatigue when I grow up. I hope my future will be better than my father's future, which was destroyed by the occupation.

My dream was to complete my education when I grew up, but the occupation destroyed dozens of universities and schools, and dozens more schools were turned into shelters for hundreds of thousands of displaced people who have lost their homes. We lost a school year from our lives. The occupation completely destroyed our lives, but I will continue to work hard to achieve my dream.

My father dreamed of rebuilding our house and maintaining a beautiful life for us, but my father is now unemployed, and the occupation completely destroyed his workplace. The responsibility now falls on me and my siblings to help our family overcome this difficult situation. I hope we can rebuild our house, and that I can contribute to providing a decent life for my younger siblings.

I often think of my martyred cousin and many of my neighbors and friends who are martyrs, and I imagine myself being targeted by the bombing soon. I could be the next martyr. I am very afraid of the sounds of shelling and gunfire, but we have become accustomed to hearing them in the eighth month of the war. I dream that the war will stop, and people will return to their home. I dream that we will return to our schools, complete our education, and end all this suffering imposed on us by the occupation. I dream that we will return to our lives, that my father will be able to find suitable work, and that smiles will return to all the children of Gaza. ♦

Over 100 Displaced People Have Sheltered in My Home Since the Beginning of the War

Rasmiyya Ahmed Abbas

❝ We still love this land, and we will never leave it. We will not emigrate from Gaza even if the occupation kills us all. We will only leave Gaza by returning to Ashdod, which was occupied in 1948 – the city from which the occupation expelled my family. We hope the war will stop, and a decent life will be found for the people of Gaza. ❞

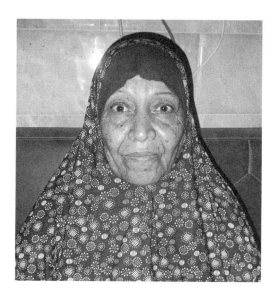

My story of hosting displaced people began at eight o'clock on the seventh day of October 2023, the first day of the Israeli war on the Gaza Strip. On that day, my daughter, her husband, their children, and the relatives of her husband who fled from the Israeli bombardment of the Shuja'iyya neighborhood in eastern Gaza City, sought refuge in my home in Nuseirat refugee camp in the central Gaza Strip. Everyone in the camp knows me by my nickname, "Um Ashraf," but few know my full name, which is Rasmiyya Ahmed Abbas, 74 years old. I was born and raised in the Beach refugee camp west of Gaza City and married Mahmoud Musa Al-Da'lasa. We lived for years in the city of Khan Younis in the southern Gaza Strip, then settled in Nuseirat camp over 30 years ago.

I managed to form rapid and meaningful relationships with all the residents of Nuseirat camp. My husband worked as the director of the Khan Younis post office in the Palestinian government, and my children are involved in trade. I am a homemaker, blessed by God with three sons, Ashraf, Mahmoud, and Hassan, and seven daughters, Manal, Niveen, Nasreen, Khatam, Eman, Rania, and Alaa. I managed to marry off all my sons and daughters, and God blessed me with many grandchildren. Currently, I live with my eldest son, Ashraf, and his children and my son Mahmoud and his children. My son Hassan traveled with his family and settled in Germany, while my daughters live with their families in various areas of the Gaza Strip.

After the Israeli occupation forces declared the southern and central Gaza Strip areas safe, dozens of displaced persons sought refuge in our four-story home in the Nuseirat camp. Each floor is about 200 square meters. One floor is for myself and my late husband, who passed away in 2021 due to COVID-19. Another floor is for Ashraf's sons, another for Mahmoud's son, and the last for Hassan, who resides outside of Palestine. The fourth floor was prepared with two fully furnished apartments for Ashraf's sons to reside in after marriage, but with the onset of the war, the entire house turned into a shelter for displaced persons.

OVER 100 DISPLACED PEOPLE SHELTERED IN MY HOME

I was very happy to provide accommodation for dozens of children, women, elders, and young people. I welcomed displaced persons from the Abbas, Tamraz, Al-Aklouk, Zaqout, Nasar, Al-Khatib, Al-Khalidi, Qoush, Atiya, Al-Arouqi, Hammad, Al-Nimnim, Jundiya, and Al-Da'lasa families. Some of these families are related to us by blood, some by marriage, and some by proximity, but all of them are connected to us through our Palestinian identity and our Islamic identity. My joy in embracing them in my home cannot be described, and with the grace of God, I have been able to fulfill this trust for the eighth consecutive month of the ongoing Israeli genocidal war on the Gaza Strip.

Among the displaced persons I've hosted in my home was one who suffered from Down syndrome and had special needs. His name was Musa Ismail Hammad, 49 years old. The occupation deprived him of his right to receive treatment since the first day of the war. The Israeli bombardment caused severe nervous breakdowns and continuous panic attacks for him. The Israeli airstrikes instilled fear in everyone, but they affected Musa even more profoundly.

We tried hard to provide treatment for Musa, but we were unsuccessful. The occupation destroyed the majority of hospitals and health centers in the Gaza Strip. Musa sought refuge in my home starting in the early days of the war, after fleeing his home in Gaza City. He suffered the consequences of the war with us, from psychological traumas to seizures and extreme fear due to the Israeli airstrikes on the Gaza Strip. We tried to support and calm him, but the occupation's missiles thwarted all our efforts. He remained in this state until he passed away due to a panic attack induced by the Israeli airstrikes. He was buried in the Nuseirat cemetery away from his home in Gaza City.

I've witnessed and lived through many painful human stories during this war, but one story that deeply affected all of us was the murder of a little girl who was not even two years old. My relatives from the Abbas family fled from the Beach refugee camp to the Nuseirat camp, and during their journey on foot, they lost their young daughter, Saja Nael Abbas, 23 years old, and her little daughter, Warda Ali Al-Nimnim, two years old. They disappeared while walking on Rashid Street, also known as Sea Street. Her family searched for them extensively but couldn't find them. Her family assumed they would reunite with them at my home, but instead slept in my house for a night without Saja and her daughter Warda.

Saja searched for her family, but as night fell, her fear grew significantly. She sought refuge in a car that had been bombed by the occupation earlier. It was pitch black, and stray dogs attacked Saja and her daughter. She hugged her daughter tightly, trying to protect her, but Saja lost consciousness from sheer terror. The next morning, she woke up to find her daughter had passed away. She suffered a severe psychological shock.

The following morning, a group of displaced persons found her sitting in a bombed car filled with the bodies of martyrs. It was very dark the night before, and Saja hadn't seen the martyrs' bodies. They found Saja crying over her deceased daughter. They asked for her name and where her family had gone. They brought her to our house, and we buried her daughter in the Nuseirat cemetery.

Saja stayed in my house for over a month. Her psychological condition was very severe. She would cry and clutch the pillow, constantly calling out for her daughter. She no longer understood what was happening around her. She attempted suicide on the rooftop of my house three times, and each time we managed to stop her. After she fled with her family to Deir al-Balah city, she attempted suicide for the fourth time, and she was rescued and prevented. However, the heinous crime she experienced robbed her of her ability to think, and she was no longer the same as before the war.

My granddaughter Raghad Mahmoud Al-Da'lasa got married to Youssef Tamraz in Jabalia refugee camp, in the north of the Gaza Strip, about six months before the war. She fled with her husband and his family to our home, then moved to their relatives' house in Deir al-Balah city. Raghad suffered greatly during pregnancy due to the difficult circumstances of the displacement journey, the long walking distances, and the lack of proper medication and food.

During their displacement in a house in Deir al-Balah city in early February 2024, Raghad experienced childbirth symptoms. Her husband searched for a midwife to assist her since the conditions at Al-Aqsa Martyrs Hospital in Deir al-Balah were catastrophic. The maternity ward had been turned into an emergency department to receive dozens of daily wounded and injured.

Her husband couldn't find a midwife, but he found a displaced nurse in a neighboring house. The nurse helped deliver my granddaughter Raghad's child, Abdulrahman, under very difficult humanitarian and health conditions.

My grandson Mohammed Ashraf Al-Da'lasa, 28 years old, got engaged to Shihada Ayman Al-Naqla a few months before the war. He built and beautifully furnished their apartment, setting Wednesday, October 11, 2023, as their wedding day and Tuesday for the bachelor party and henna night. He printed wedding invitations and distributed them to relatives, neighbors, and friends. He reserved the bride's dress and the wedding hall, completing all the details and requirements for the celebration.

We were very happy for our first grandson Mohammed to get married, but the war began on Saturday, October 7, 2023, and we postponed the wedding due to the harsh war conditions. Mohammed's apartment, which had been prepared for the wedding, was turned into a shelter for dozens of displaced persons. Likewise, the apartment of Musa, his brother, which had been prepared for his upcoming wedding, also became a shelter for the displaced. As the war continued, the bombings intensified, and we lost many martyrs, we decided to marry Mohammed despite the war.

In mid-November, after a month of the Israeli war on the Gaza Strip, my son Ashraf, his wife, my son Mahmoud, and I went to the bride's family's house. The groom Mohammed took his bride Shihada without any wedding ceremonies, festivities, or the usual customs and traditions we're accustomed to. There was no room for joy in the Gaza Strip. The occupation brought sadness into every Palestinian home in the Strip.

After three months of ongoing war in Gaza, we experienced the suffering of displacement like the rest of the Gaza Strip residents. The Israeli forces stormed the camps of the central governorate, including Nuseirat, Bureij, and Maghazi, and we were forced to evacuate our home for the first time during the war. My sons asked me to evacuate with them to outside Nuseirat. I initially refused to leave my home, but after their insistence, I went with them.

I fled with my son Ashraf and his family to my granddaughter's house in the Sawarha area of Al-Zawayda village, south of Nuseirat camp. The number of displaced persons in my granddaughter's small house exceeded 25, most of them children and women. We stayed with them for about a month, then returned to our house in Nuseirat camp.

Upon our return, we were shocked by the extensive damage to our house caused by the Israeli shelling. Several neighboring houses were destroyed, including the five-story house of Dr. Anwar Qoush and a nearby charitable women's association. These homes were completely destroyed, and about 20 people, mostly children and displaced persons, were killed. The Israeli shelling also caused severe damage to our house, breaking windows and doors, and causing significant structural damage.

As we returned home, dozens of displaced relatives, friends, and neighbors who had also lost their homes due to the Israeli shelling also returned with us. We repaired what we could of the house, and covered the windows with nylon and blankets. Had we been at home during the bombing, everyone would have been killed. My sons found the remains of a child martyr from the Shabrawi family on the balcony of my son Mahmoud's apartment. The area was completely devastated.

Now, I live in a damaged house with my sons, daughters, grandchildren, and dozens of displaced persons. The house remains open to all displaced persons, despite all the Israeli bombing that has struck Gaza for nearly the past eight months. We still love this land, and we will never leave it. We will not emigrate from Gaza even if the occupation kills us all. We will only leave Gaza by returning to Ashdod, which was occupied in 1948 – the city from which the occupation expelled my family. We hope the war will stop, and a decent life will be found for the people of Gaza. We hope the occupation will be held accountable for the hundreds of genocidal crimes committed in Gaza.

I have lived through all the wars that Gaza has faced except for the Nakba war, but I have never seen anything like this war in terms of killing, destruction, and genocide. We love our homeland, and we will never leave it. ◆

My Mother Returned Home to Die: The Injustices Against Elderly Patients in the Gaza Strip

Ali Al-Owisi

> ❝ We cried with my mother every time. She cried from pain and agony, and we cried from our helplessness and inability to provide assistance, medication, or relieve her pain. My mother suffered all the time, and our hearts were crushed with pain. This is our mother whom we love dearly, whom we do not want to lose, and who loves life and wants to continue it with us in good health. ❞

My name is Ali al-Owisi, and I am 29 years old. My mother spent her last days in great agony. She's spent the last two years unable to walk, and fell into a coma for a week before dying, affected by kidney failure and cancer. Her pain increased, with no painkillers or medications to alleviate her suffering. She couldn't eat, so we fed her through medical injections. These are my mother's final days.

My mother's name was Raghdah Ali al-Owisi. She lived to be 71 years old, and was born in the city of Rafah in the southern Gaza Strip. But her family was from the town of Zarnouqa, which was occupied in 1948. She married my father, Hassan al-Owisi, at the age of 24, and gave birth to three sons, Fadi, Ibrahim, and me, Ali, and three daughters, Huda, Maha, and Asma. She was a grandmother to 20 grandchildren and lived with them in the Nuseirat refugee camp in the middle of the Gaza Strip, where our family home was located. Our lives were happy with our parents.

In 2021, after many rounds of medical examinations, we discovered my mother suffered from kidney failure. We tried every possible way to treat her. The doctors prescribed weekly kidney dialysis sessions at the Al-Aqsa Martyrs Hospital in the city of Deir al-Balah in the middle of the Gaza Strip.

At the beginning of her illness, the doctors prescribed three weekly kidney dialysis sessions, each lasting for four continuous hours. My mother endured it, trying to hide her pain from us, but the pain was too great to hide or for her to bear. I had never seen my mother cry before. Among us, she lived a happy, peaceful life, but during her illness, I saw her tears many times. The pain and suffering took all her energy.

My mother dreamed of traveling and undergoing kidney transplant surgeries. We all agreed to donate a kidney to her if we could. My mother tried her best to be patient, believing that she might be able to travel soon, live her life normally, and overcome the disease. Dialysis sessions began with high spirits and great faith in a complete and quick recovery.

A year after starting the kidney dialysis sessions, my mother's health deteriorated, and she became unable to walk. We were forced to transfer her to the hospital in an ambulance dedicated to kidney dialysis. My brothers and I took turns leaving our work so that one of us could accompany our mother to each kidney dialysis session.

The process of transferring my mother to the hospital for kidney dialysis required great effort. My mother lived on the second floor of our house and couldn't walk. We worked together with the ambulance driver, the nurse, and the neighbors to lift my mother and transfer her to the ambulance and back to the second floor after each kidney dialysis session. We hoped that our mother would recover with treatment and that the treatment would alleviate her pain.

My mother remained committed to her kidney dialysis sessions at the Al-Aqsa Martyrs Hospital until the Israeli war on Gaza broke out on the seventh of October, 2023. After thousands of families were displaced from Gaza City and the northern governorate of the Strip, the number of kidney patients in the dialysis department at the Al-Aqsa Martyrs Hospital increased significantly, greatly affecting my mother and all the other patients.

The kidney dialysis department has 22 kidney dialysis machines, some of which are out of order and not functioning. The department provides medical services to 140 kidney failure patients from the central governorate of the Gaza Strip. However, during the war, the department began providing services to 480 patients after many residents in Gaza were displaced.

The pressure from the large number of patients on the kidney failure department exceeded the hospital's management capabilities. The hospital administration appealed daily to international institutions and the international community to provide kidney dialysis machines to save the lives of kidney failure patients in the Gaza Strip, but their calls and pleas went unanswered.

In early January 2024, Israeli forces stormed the camps in the middle of the Gaza Strip, including the one we lived in, the Nuseirat camp, and we were forced to flee to Rafah city to my uncle's house. We couldn't afford an ambulance to transport my mother, and they were all occupied anyway transporting the wounded and the martyrs. We transported my mother in a car.

We were staying about 60 kilometers [37.3 miles] from Rafah city, only a half an hour away. But I felt the distance was hours longer. My mother's moans and cries of pain never stopped due to her deteriorating health condition and her uncomfortable sleeping position in the car. But we had no choice. The shelling reached all areas in the Nuseirat camp, and we fled with my mother out of fear of death.

My uncle's house is in the Saudi neighborhood west of Rafah city, but the Abu Yousef Al-Najjar Hospital, which has a kidney dialysis department, is located in the eastern areas of Rafah city. Since we couldn't afford an ambulance to transport my mother, we transported her in a private car at our own expense, which cost us between 200 and 300 shekels for each kidney dialysis session.

The kidney dialysis department at this hospital was small and overcrowded with patients. The majority of kidney failure patients in the Gaza Strip now undergo dialysis there, as it is the only hospital still operating in the southern Gaza Strip. The department lacked cleanliness due to the harsh war conditions that destroyed the healthcare system in all governorates of the Gaza Strip.

We stayed in Rafah city for a month, but after the occupation withdrew from the camps in the middle of the Strip, my mother insisted we return to our home in Nuseirat camp. The journey back home was like continuous torment. My mother's pains never stopped, and her tears never ceased.

We cried with my mother every time. She cried from pain and agony, and we cried from our helplessness and inability to provide assistance, medication, or relieve her pain. My mother suffered all the time, and our hearts were crushed with pain. This is our mother whom we love dearly, whom we do not want to lose, and who loves life and wants to continue it with us in good health. However, the occupation had a different idea. The war created a harsh reality for the patients of Gaza.

My mother's health deteriorated after our return to the Nuseirat camp. She couldn't even enter the bathroom. There was no electricity or water for more than six months in Gaza. My mother wore diapers. We bought painkillers even if we could only find them at high prices, but they did not save her life.

During Ramadan of this year, doctors discovered that my mother had cancer in her abdomen and the lower part of her body. This filled us with extreme fear and panic. My mother's body couldn't resist kidney failure, so how would she cope with the deadly cancer as well? We didn't tell her for fear of upsetting her. We told her that the pain in her abdomen and lower body was due to the complications of kidney failure.

She fell into a coma for a week, and we couldn't find a place for her in the hospital. Our mother remained in a coma at our home for a week. The doctors took turns checking on her, but my mother died at home, affected by her kidney failure that lasted for three years and the cancer we discovered a month before her death. My mother died on Wednesday, May 29, 2024, due to the occupation's unjust policy toward patients in Gaza, depriving them of their right to treatment, destroying the healthcare system in the Strip, and causing the deaths of dozens of patients due to oppression, pain, and deprivation of treatment.

We couldn't find enough space in the cemetery to bury my mother, so we dug up my grandmother's grave and buried my mother in the same grave. There is no space in the cemetery to bury our deceased due to the large number of martyrs who have fallen during this war. My mother responded to treatment before the war broke out, but the war reset her health to zero. Physical therapy sessions and painkillers failed to relieve her pain and agony. She suffered greatly for more than six months during the war. My mother died complaining to God about the injustice of the occupation and the world's abandonment of the suffering patients in Gaza ♦

The Need to Obtain Water Is the Greatest Suffering We Are Exposed to in the Displacement Tents

Nidaa Abu Toha

> In our home, we had four bathrooms. Today we have none. We live in a tent, and when we need to use the bathroom, we go to the schools set up as shelters for displaced people. We line up in long queues to enter bathrooms with no water.

THERE is no water in the shelters. All the water wells in the UNRWA schools and Palestinian government schools, which have become shelters for tens of thousands of displaced people, are not functioning. There is barely any fuel. The Rafah and Karim Abu Salem crossings, which were used to transport fuel to operate our water wells, are closed. The only operating well is in Khan Younis city, where I, displaced, now live. I go to the well every day to fill a 20-liter gallon of water. This is a daily challenge. I can handle hunger, but I need water to survive, maintain hygiene, and cook.

Under normal circumstances, my family's daily water requirement is about 20 liters per person. Today, I share 20 liters of water among 23 family members. We make great efforts to conserve water, as we do not have our own bathroom. We live in a tent for the displaced, and we use a public bathroom, which lacks cleanliness and water. But we are forced to live this way. We face a continual threat of disease, with no way to combat it due to the water shortage.

I have two children, Saif al-Din al-Masri, 12 years old, and Adam al-Masri, three-and-a-half years old. I divorced my husband three years ago, and I live in a small room with my children in my family's house in Shati refugee camp west of Gaza City. Before the war, I searched extensively for a job to support my children, but I couldn't find one. There are no job opportunities in the Gaza Strip. Most of the population suffers from extreme poverty.

My family's displacement journey began on Tuesday, November 7, 2023, after the Israeli bombardment intensified on Shati refugee camp. On the fifth day of the Israeli occupation's ground operation in the Gaza Strip, the Israeli incursion focused on Gaza City and the northern Strip, bombing dozens of buildings adjacent to my family's house, and forcing us to leave our refugee camp under heavy bombardment.

I ran with my son Saif al-Din, gripping my youngest, Adam. I tried to protect them from the scattered Israeli shelling. There was shrapnel everywhere. The occupation forces asked us to head to the southern areas of the Gaza Valley, and my father decided that we would evacuate to Khan Younis city. We walked long distances on foot as the occupation stopped the entry of fuel and petroleum on October 7, 2023, preventing us from being able to use a car. The walk is 40 kilometers [24.9 miles] from our home in Shati refugee camp.

My father bought a small tent for us and placed it near the Nasser Medical Complex in Khan Younis city. We stayed there for over a month. We fled again under bombardment after the occupation invaded Khan Younis city at the beginning of December 2023. We were horrified by how close the occupation's tanks were to us, but we miraculously escaped from them while raising white flags.

We then fled to Rafah city, where we stayed in tents, then returned to Khan Younis city a week after the occupation invaded the eastern areas of Rafah city. We are still living in tents. The war is ongoing, and we are still deprived of living in our home.

The third day of January 2024 will remain etched in my mind forever. On this day, the occupation forces bombed my family's house in the Shati refugee camp and destroyed it. I lived in this house with 23 family members, and today we are all displaced, living in tents. Our lives were tied to our house and living in Shati refugee camp, but now, for the seventh month, we are strangers to our home. We suffer from a lack of the necessities of life.

Thirteen children lived in my father's house, all under the age of ten. They are now living in difficult conditions in tents. Their crying continues throughout the day. We can barely provide a meal for them, and even the meal we provide is insufficient and unsatisfactory for them. We live on aid, and the aid we receive is very limited. The conditions of the displaced in the tents are extremely difficult.

In our home, we had four bathrooms. Today we have none. We live in a tent, and when we need to use the bathroom, we go to the schools set up as shelters for displaced people. We line up in long queues to enter bathrooms with no water. I am afraid for myself and my children. I am afraid of diseases and the spread of epidemics due to the health hazards and waste everywhere in the Gaza Strip.

We currently live in a tent near the Sheikh Jameel School, which belongs to UNRWA in Khan Younis city. We are exposed to the danger of bombing at all times.

My family, like all families in the Gaza Strip, has suffered from the loss of many family members. My cousin's son was martyred while he was in a barber shop near the Israa School in the Shati refugee camp. He wanted to cut his hair, but the occupation deprived him of his life while he was waiting for his turn in the barber shop. In this assassination, dozens of others were also martyred and injured.

The occupation bombed my uncle's house, and his wife, Abeer Abu Toha, 42, was martyred in the bombing, as well as his son Ahmed Abu Toha, 14, and his grandson, the child Ahmed Heid, who was two-and-a-half years old. The occupation killed them in a heinous crime, destroyed their house completely, and my uncle's children lost their mother forever.

The occupation's crimes are not limited to my family alone. The occupation has ruined all Palestinian homes. Many of my friends, neighbors, and relatives have been killed. Many of my son Saif al-Din's classmates have been killed. Many children that were the same age as my three-year-old son Adam have been killed, and some even younger than him. The occupation has committed hundreds of crimes during its more than seven-month-long continuous war on the Gaza Strip. The Israeli war machine continues to kill more innocent people.

My son Saif al-Din lost both his cousin and his friend Ahmed as martyrs during the war. My son used to play with Ahmed every day and loved him dearly. Saif al-Din can't stop remembering him and mourning him. He continues to cry whenever he remembers him and asks me, "Why did the occupation kill my friend Ahmed? What did Ahmed do to the occupation to be killed?" The occupation's crimes have affected all inhabitants of the Gaza Strip.

My children wake up terrified from the sound of bombing. We live in a cloth tent, and our lives are at risk all the time, especially from shrapnel that falls during nearby bombings. Recently, shrapnel fell on our tent. I tried to calm my children down and tell them that the bombing was far away, but they hear the sounds all the time. The bombing has not stopped in the Gaza Strip since the beginning of the war.

My son Adam was supposed to start kindergarten next year, but now he helps us carry water and gather food distributions. The occupation deprived my children of their childhood and deprived them of living in safety and peace. My children only get one meal a day. They sleep all day hungry, but this is the situation for all the inhabitants of the Gaza Strip.

Our dream is to get food and water daily, to return to our house in Shati refugee camp, and to be able to rebuild it. I dream of educating my children and creating a beautiful future for them. My children fled from Khan Younis city in front of the occupation tanks and under intense bombing. My only wish is for the war to stop and for us to return to our lives, for Gaza to be rebuilt, and for us to live in peace and security like the rest of the world's population. ♦

My Husband Was Martyred While Searching for Food for Us

Najlaa Al-Kafarna

❝ The occupation has completely destroyed the healthcare system in the Gaza Strip, and there are no functioning hospitals where treatment is available for Muhammad. Muhammad is five years old and weighs no more than ten kilograms [22 pounds], a weight that is not proportional to his age. His mental capacity is also much lower than his age. ❞

I GOT married seven years ago to Jihad Adnan Al-Kafarna. We were married in a small room in his family's house in Beit Hanoun, in the north of the Gaza Strip, and lived a beautiful life together. Shortly after we got married, we built two rooms, a kitchen, and a

MY HUSBAND WAS MARTYRED SEARCHING FOR FOOD

bathroom of our own. God blessed us with three children: Adnan, six years old; Muhammad, five years old; and Adam, one year old. Our children were the main source of joy in our lives, and we were happy to live together in Beit Hanoun, where we were both born and raised. Our hearts were attached to Beit Hanoun, and we only left there when it became necessary. But now, we have been living far away from Beit Hanoun for nearly eight months due to the Israeli war on the Gaza Strip.

Before the war, I lived with my family in our house located on Atiya Al-Za'anin Street, in the Safiya area of Beit Hanoun. My son Muhammad was born with a permanent physical disability and requires special medical care. We have worked to provide care for him for the past five years.

We were displaced from our home on the second day of the war on Gaza – on October 8, 2023. My husband, children, and I left Beit Hanoun for the Jabalia camp. We stayed in Abu Zeitoun School, affiliated with UNRWA. Our house was completely destroyed in the early days of the war.

We fled, surrounded by the occupation's shells and missiles. We walked for over ten kilometers [6.2 miles] until we reached Jabalia camp, where we spent our first day in the school-turned-shelter without food. We slept on the floor without blankets. My husband went out on the second day after our arrival to search for food and drink for us. The Israeli shelling on Jabalia camp was very intense.

I asked my husband to take care of himself and to stay away from the shelling areas. He told me that he would go to Jabalia camp market to get some food. About an hour after my husband left, I heard other displaced people in the school talking about Israeli shelling on Jabalia market. I started to feel extreme fear, and my heart began to beat fast. I tried to call my husband repeatedly, but the network was busy. My brothers went out to search for him, and they returned in the evening with sad faces. I knew that the situation was serious, but I didn't think that I had lost my husband.

I ran toward my brothers and asked about my husband. They told me that he had been martyred in the Israeli shelling on Jabalia camp market on October 9, 2023. He was martyred in a shelling that resulted in a large massacre, in which dozens were killed or wounded. My husband was martyred on the third day of the war, leaving me alone with the responsibility of raising three children. This news was harsh, as I couldn't even bid farewell to my husband. My brothers buried him in Jabalia camp cemetery without me being able to kiss him goodbye. They had to bury him quickly because of the intensity of the Israeli shelling that targeted all areas.

After my husband's martyrdom, I lost the support I relied on for every aspect of my life. With the intensification of the shelling on Jabalia camp, I fled with my elderly father to Beit Lahia. We stayed in UNRWA schools-turned-shelters for three days, but the area was also subjected to intense Israeli shelling. We then evacuated to the UNRWA health center "Jabalia Clinic" in Jabalia camp, where we stayed for three days. Due to the intensified shelling on Jabalia camp, we left the northern Gaza Strip and headed south to Wadi Gaza, as requested by the occupation forces, as the southern Wadi areas were supposed to be safe.

We arrived in Khan Younis, in the southern Gaza Strip, after a long journey of suffering, during which we walked several kilometers on foot. We lived in a relative's house. However, after a few days, the occupation bombed the house adjacent to ours, causing significant damage to the house we had evacuated to. My father asked us to leave Khan Younis and head to another, safer area. Our only goal was to search for safety for ourselves and our children.

We left Khan Younis and headed to the Nuseirat camp in the central Gaza Strip. We stayed in Mamdouh Saeedam School with thousands of other displaced people in tents for two months. In early January 2024, the occupation planes dropped leaflets on us demanding the evacuation of Nuseirat camp. We immediately evacuated Nuseirat camp and headed to the tents for displaced people

MY HUSBAND WAS MARTYRED SEARCHING FOR FOOD

in Deir al-Balah. We have now been living in tents in the Akila area for the fifth consecutive month. Thousands of tents surround us on all sides. Tens of thousands of families live in adjacent tents. We are all seeking safety and constantly fleeing from the Israeli shelling, but it chases us wherever we flee.

I had not yet recovered from the news of my husband's martyrdom when I received news of the martyrdom of several of my relatives. My husband's sister, Ghada Adnan Al-Kafarna, 46 years old, was martyred along with her sons: Mohammed, 29 years old; Anas, 23 years old; and Ramiz, 18 years old. My husband's other sister, Najwa, 47 years old, was martyred along with her son Ahmed, 32 years old. They were all martyred in the same massacre in which my husband was martyred, the shelling on Jabalia camp market. In the massacre, I lost my husband and six of my relatives. They were all searching for food, fleeing from death, but the occupation's missiles pursued them everywhere, taking their lives and depriving us of their beautiful presence in our lives. I lost my husband and six of my relatives in a single Israeli bombing.

The bombing that damaged the house we had evacuated to in Khan Younis resulted in injuries to my siblings. My brother Mahmoud, 23 years old, suffered bruises on his body. My sister Sajja, 19 years old, suffered severe burns on her body. My sister Fatima, 16 years old, suffered injuries and burns all over her body. My sister Aya, six years old, suffered bruises on her body. They stayed in Nasser Medical Complex in Khan Younis for several days and then joined us in the tents of Nuseirat camp, fleeing with us to the tents in Deir al-Balah.

Five years ago, Allah blessed me with my son Muhammad. Muhammad was born with cerebral atrophy, delayed motor skills, and significant cognitive impairments. Doctors informed me that he would require constant treatment, including regular physical therapy sessions, medical supplements, and ongoing medical monitoring. However, since the beginning of the war, Muhammad has been deprived of his treatment. He has lived with us in the displacement tents, fleeing from the occupation's missiles in Jabalia camp, Beit Lahia, Khan Younis, and Nuseirat. Now, we are enduring hardship in Deir al-Balah.

We don't have the financial means to support the specialized treatment for my disabled son. On the first day of the war, we lost contact with the physical therapy team that had been treating Muhammad. The occupation has completely destroyed the healthcare system in the Gaza Strip, and there are barely any functioning hospitals where treatment is available for Muhammad. Muhammad is five years old and weighs no more than ten kilograms [22 pounds], a weight that is not proportional to his age. His mental capacity is also much lower than his age.

I am always thinking about how to care best for my son Muhammad and how to provide what he needs. Muhammad needs diapers constantly, along with his specific medications and ongoing physical therapy sessions. He has required physical and mental therapy since birth. He needs dairy products, milk, and nutritional supplements rich in vitamins. He needs prescription glasses to correct his vision deviation. We need personal hygiene products for all of us.

However, I am confronted with the reality of what we are currently living through. We have lost everything because of the war. The occupation deprived my children of their father, bombed and destroyed our home, deprived my children of their right to live in a safe place, and deprived my disabled son Muhammad of his right to treatment. The occupation has deprived us of everything and destroyed our lives.

We have been living in tents for nearly eight months, and life in the tents is very sad. There is no water, and we cannot always find food. We eat only one meal a day, which is not enough. The temperatures are very high, and there are no sewage networks. Sewage and waste spread everywhere, and the foul odors are harmful. We face difficulty in providing for our daily needs. We live in an unhealthy and unsuitable environment, which poses many risks to my life and the lives of my children.

We were almost hit by the Israeli shelling near the tents. A house in Deir al-Balah next to the tents we live in was bombed, causing stones to fall on us. My brother was preparing food when the stones fell on the pot in which the food was being prepared, causing burns on his body from the boiling water. Danger follows us everywhere.

Miraculously, we survived after the occupation bombed the Al-Astal family's house while we were displaced in Khan Younis. Civil defense and ambulance men managed to evacuate us from the shelling area and took us to Nasser Hospital. From there, we fled to Nuseirat camp. All this suffering, and I am responsible for three children alone, including a disabled child who needs to be carried constantly. ♦

The Occupation Killed Every Member of My Family by Bombing Our Home

Mohammed Ali Al-Bibi

❝ We lived in the center for three weeks in extreme danger. The occupation vehicles came very close to the school, and quadcopter drones roamed inside the school and fired at anyone moving. My sister's husband Mohammed, Adham, and I were shelled with an artillery shell while baking bread in the schoolyard. We left the bread and ran into the classrooms, and by God's grace, we survived the shelling. ❞

THE crime committed by the occupation forces against my family is not unique among the thousands of crimes inflicted on the

THE OCCUPATION KILLED EVERY MEMBER OF MY FAMILY

Palestinian people since the occupation of Palestine in 1948. However, the crimes committed during this war are particularly massive and heinous, beyond description. I've lost everything beautiful in this war. I've lost every member of my family and my home. Now, I am all alone, without family, friends, or a home.

This is a summary of my experience during this war. I am Mohammed Ali Al-Bibi, a 17-year-old, tenth-grade student. I used to live with my family in our house in the Zaytoun neighborhood of Gaza City. Our life was peaceful and beautiful before the war, but now everything has changed, and I've lost everything I had.

My story began when my sister, Zuhwa, called me. She and her family had fled in the early days of the Israeli war on Gaza to an UNRWA school turned into a shelter for displaced people in the Nuseirat camp. They fled after their house was bombed and completely destroyed by the occupation. She asked me to bring diapers and some necessities for her baby daughter. I got what she needed and set out from our house in Gaza City to the Nuseirat camp on foot.

The Israeli occupation forces were stationed near the Martyrs' Junction on Salah al-Din Street, dividing Gaza into two sections. I passed by the occupation vehicles while carrying a white piece of cloth and the diapers and milk for my niece. I saw many bodies lying on the ground and witnessed dozens of martyrs. The occupation allowed some civilians, including me, to pass, subjecting us to thorough inspection.

After a difficult journey, I reached the school-turned-shelter and gave my sister the supplies for her baby daughter. On the same day, I returned to Salah al-Din Street to go back to my home and family in the Zaytoun neighborhood. However, the occupation forces prevented us from passing and fired bullets at us, instructing us to return from another street. When we arrived four kilometers [2.5 miles] away on foot, the occupation forces prevented us from passing again. So I returned to my sister at the school-turned-shelter in the Nuseirat camp.

My brother Ismail had arrived at the school in Nuseirat a few days before my sister. In late December 2023, Ismail left the school-turned-shelter and headed to the Malaysian Quranic school on the northern outskirts of the Nuseirat camp, wanting to be closer to Gaza City.

Every day, Ismail tried to return to Gaza City, but the occupation forces fired at him. They had infiltrated the Magra'ah area and the entire Zahraa neighborhood. Despite this, Ismail was deeply connected to our mother and siblings and wanted to return to our family.

Occupation forces on the outskirts of Wadi Gaza fired directly at Ismail, aged 20, and my cousin Khamees Ahmed Al-Bibi, aged 23, on their last attempt to return to Gaza City. Khamees was killed instantly by a bullet to his chest and was identified by the ID card he had in his pocket.

My cousin Khamees was buried, but for the past five months, we have heard nothing about my brother Ismail. Some say he was martyred and buried in the sands after the northern Nuseirat area was raided and the Malaysian school destroyed. Others say he was detained by the occupation forces. I search for Ismail every day, but I know nothing about him. I hope he is still alive, and we can continue our lives together.

I communicated with my family through mobile phones, but connecting was difficult due to heavy blockage on the mobile network. I bought a SIM card from a national company, but still, communicating with my family was very difficult. My mother constantly reassured me, asking me to stay in the school and take care of myself. But the occupation's missiles killed my mother, and everyone else in my family.

On Tuesday, February 20, 2024, the occupation forces bombed my family's house in the Zaytoun neighborhood, destroying it. All the members of my family were martyred. The occupation killed my father, Mohammed Ali Al-Bibi, 44 years old; my mother, Mona Al-Zarad, 42 years old; my brother Ali, 24 years old; my brother

Ayman, 14 years old; and my brother Zaher, ten years old. Also martyred in the bombing were my uncle Ahmed Al-Bibi's family, including his wife and their sons, Mohammed, 18 years old, and Saqr, 12 years old.

The occupation committed a large massacre by bombing our house in the Zaytoun neighborhood. Everyone in my family home was a civilian, and there is no justification for the occupation to have committed such a heinous crime against them. I lost my entire family and was left alone. Due to poor communication, I only learned about my family's martyrdom ten days after the occupation's crime. Since then, I have been suffering from severe psychological shock. I cannot comprehend how to continue my life alone. I couldn't bid them farewell or participate in their burial. The occupation killed the entire rest of my family, and I still don't know whether my brother Ismail was killed or arrested. I live in constant worry and in a bad mental state.

Since January, I have been living with my sister Zuhwa, 26 years old; her husband Mohammed; and their children: Sabah, eight years old; Mona, six years old; Rahef, three years old; and the infant Aziz, ten months old, who was born shortly before the war. We are all displaced, as the occupation destroyed our homes and killed our family.

My sister and her children sleep in one of the school's classrooms along with about ten other families. My sister's husband sleeps with the men in a separate building designated for them. I couldn't find a space for myself to sleep in the men's building, so I sleep in a tent in the school-turned-shelter's courtyard. We are facing difficult living conditions. We need water, food, and cleaning supplies. We need everything, but we only have a small mattress and blanket shared by multiple people for sleeping.

The school-turned-shelter's management distributes food assistance to us, but it is minimal. They distribute only one bar of soap per family, which is not sufficient. We don't have clean water, and we don't have clothes. We have been wearing the same clothes we were displaced in months ago. We have been wearing these clothes throughout autumn and winter, and now throughout spring.

When the occupation forces invaded the central Gaza camps in early January 2024, most families living in the school-turned-shelter left and fled to Deir al-Balah and the southern Gaza Strip. However, we refused to be displaced again for several reasons. First, we didn't want to face displacement again, and second, we didn't have the money to move to another place. We decided to stay inside the school-turned-shelter despite the great danger we faced.

We lived in the center for three weeks in extreme danger. The occupation vehicles came very close to the school, and quadcopter drones roamed inside the school and fired at anyone moving. My sister's husband Mohammed, Adham, and I were shelled with an artillery shell while baking bread in the schoolyard. We left the bread and ran into the classrooms, and by God's grace, we survived the shelling.

During those three weeks, we couldn't find enough food. Our neighbors would send us whatever was left of their food. We couldn't find flour, and we couldn't find water for drinking or other uses. We lived for three weeks without food or drink, which was very harsh on us, especially on the children. We have been short of flour since the beginning of the war, barely managing to provide one meal a day for ourselves. We bake over the fire, but the amount of bread is insufficient due to the scarcity of flour. We try to ration its use so that one bag of flour lasts for several days.

Before the war, I was a student in the tenth grade, and after school, I used to work with my father in the tailoring profession. In this way, I helped him with household expenses. However, I lost my job during the war. We also lost my father and all the other members of my family. I worked briefly in the Nuseirat camp in a meat shop, but after the camp was invaded, the employer fled to Rafah, and I lost my job. Currently, I live only on humanitarian aid like the rest of the residents of the Gaza Strip.

My dream is to continue my education and return to my home in Gaza City. I hope to find the burial place of my family and visit

THE OCCUPATION KILLED EVERY MEMBER OF MY FAMILY

their graves as soon as I return to the Zaytoun neighborhood. I dream of finding my brother Ismail alive. Many people tell me he was martyred, but I feel he is still alive, and I hope he is. I hope to be able to rebuild our house and start a family. I will have children whom I will name after my father, mother, and martyred siblings.

Since the martyrdom of my family, I have been in a bad mental state, losing focus and suffering from nervous shock. I wish everything I've been through was just a dream, and I could wake up to find my family with me. I can't believe everything that has happened, and I no longer comprehend reality. My last communication with my family was a week before their martyrdom, and I lost my phone after their death. I sleep in a tent for displaced people. The war must stop, and the occupation must be held accountable for its heinous crime against my family. ♦

Displaced in 1948 and Today, Surviving Another Nakba and Genocide

Mohammed Abdul Jabbar Abu Seif

> I am an old man, 91 years old, suffering from diseases, but my testament to my children and grandchildren is to never leave Gaza. We cannot leave Gaza, and we cannot migrate again. In 1948, we left our homes out of fear of death. After nearly eight months of war on Gaza in 2023 and 2024, we will stay on our land until death.

I WAS 15 years old during the occupation of Palestine in 1948. I was aware of all the developments of the Israeli war and Israel's occupation of the entire Palestinian land. At that time, the targets of the occupation were specific, and we did not have the weapons to confront and expel the occupation from our land. But this war, ongoing for nearly eight months, is the toughest, harshest, and largest. For nearly the past eight months, we have been subjected to bombardment with thousands of tons of explosives. This war is larger than the 1948 Nakba. I am 91 years old. My name is Mohammed Abdul Jabbar Abu Seif.

The objectives of the occupation during the 1948 war were few, limited, and concentrated in specific areas. But in this war, the occupation's objective is to destroy the Gaza Strip. The 1948 war covered the entire area of Palestine, while this war covers a small area not exceeding 360 square kilometers [139 square miles]. This war has been the toughest period for us since the occupation of Palestine.

I am one of the few Nakba survivors still alive. The majority of my generation who lived through the catastrophe in 1948 have either died or been killed by the occupation. My family and I were expelled from the village of Julis 76 years ago, after which we endured a difficult displacement journey. We migrated to several Palestinian cities, fleeing from shelling until we reached the Bureij camp in the middle of the Gaza Strip, where we settled for several years. We then lived in the Nuseirat camp for more than 60 years.

I arrived in the Gaza Strip as a teenager and endured all the suffering of displacement with my family. We walked on foot for tens of kilometers and suffered greatly in the early years of displacement. We slept in the open, then in dilapidated tents, then in mud houses, and finally in houses made of asbestos, tiles, and stones. A few years ago, we managed to build concrete houses. Our lives were miserable, lacking all the necessities of life, but we were committed to staying in Palestine and never migrating from it.

I got married in 1955 according to Palestinian customs and traditions. My wife gave birth to six children, four daughters, and two sons, and my children collectively gave birth to 46 grandchildren. Most of my grandchildren received higher education and worked as engineers, doctors, teachers, and in many other jobs that served our people in the Gaza Strip. This service confirms our determination to continue living on this land and our refusal to leave it except by returning to our village of Julis, which was occupied in 1948.

I am an old man, 91 years old, suffering from diseases, but my testament to my children and grandchildren is to never leave Gaza. We cannot leave Gaza, and we cannot migrate again. In 1948, we left our homes out of fear of death. After nearly eight months of war on Gaza in 2023 and 2024, we will stay on our land until death. We remain steadfast due to our awareness and understanding of all the conspiracies of the occupation, and our insistence on staying in Gaza and not migrating from it, no matter what sacrifices it costs us.

I did not leave my house during the first three months of the Israeli war on the Gaza Strip. The area surrounding my house, located in the Abu Halou area in the middle of the Nuseirat refugee camp, was subjected to intense Israeli shelling. Dozens of my neighbors and loved ones were martyred, and hundreds were injured by the occupation. However, I refused to leave my home because I did not want to experience displacement again.

The occupation destroyed the nearby Ahmed Yassin Mosque, where I used to perform all my prayers. They also demolished dozens of houses adjacent to mine and shelled the land next to my house numerous times. My house has been significantly damaged, with fragments of the occupation's rockets penetrating it. My children asked me to leave the house, but I refused and insisted on staying in my home. I want to die in my house, and I do not want to die while being displaced for the second time. This option is unacceptable to me.

After the occupation invaded the central camps of the Gaza Strip in mid-January 2024, most residents of the Nuseirat camp fled to Deir al-Balah and Rafah in the southern Gaza Strip. I moved with my children to Rafah and lived in tents for a full month. It felt like a second migration, reminiscent of my displacement in 1948. I could not sleep during this period. I have now also lived through this war in 2023/2024, which is unprecedented.

Upon returning, I found my house severely damaged, so my children took me to my daughter's house in the middle of the camp. I have been living with my daughter and grandchildren as a displaced person for over three months. I miss my house and the neighborhood where I live. I cannot become a refugee again. We cannot make Israel's plan of depopulating Gaza successful. We must thwart the occupation's plans and remain steadfast on our land despite the great killing perpetrated by the occupation since the beginning of the war.

The war waged by the occupation on Gaza since October 2023 is the toughest. I have never seen such a war in my life. I lived through the 1948 war, the 1956 war, the occupation of the Gaza Strip, the Naksa of 1967, the 1973 war, the first Intifada in 1987, the second Intifada in 2000, the 2006 war, the 2008/2009 war, the 2012 war, the 2014 war, the 2021 war, and many other major Israeli attacks during its occupation of Palestine. I have now also lived during this war in 2023/2024, but this war is unprecedented.

For several months, we have been experiencing a war of extermination and destruction of humans and nature. It is a war whose objective is ethnic cleansing, ending the Palestinian cause, and expelling the Palestinian people from their land. The destructive power with which the occupation bombs all areas of the Gaza Strip is unprecedented in the history of the occupation of Palestine.

I have now lived through all the wars of the occupation. The defeat of the Arab armies lasted only six days in the Naksa of 1967. However, the occupation has been bombing Gaza for nearly eight months, and its forces have entered many areas in the Strip. The occupation has succeeded in killing and injuring over 100,000 Palestinians and destroying over 70% of Gaza's homes. It has managed to force people into tents. The occupation is waging a war of extermination against more than two million Palestinians, but we are still clinging to our land, and we will not leave it no matter what happens.

During the early days of the war, I was in constant communication with my cousin Mukhtar Abu Kaed Abu Seif, 73 years old, who is a resident of Gaza City. He refused to leave Gaza City and resisted evacuation. He remained steadfast in his home until the occupation tanks reached his house.

The occupation forces stormed the house of my cousin Mukhtar Abu Kaed in November 2023 and arrested him, along with many of his sons and neighbors. The occupation used my elderly cousin as a human shield, parading him around the neighborhoods of Gaza City. These scenes remind us of the Nakba. Generations have changed, but the Israeli criminal mentality remains the same.

The occupation demanded that my cousin Mukhtar Abu Kaed ask people to leave Gaza City and evacuate to areas south of the Gaza Valley. The occupation forces entered many neighborhoods in Gaza City using my cousin as a human shield. After that, we have no information about him. We do not know if he was killed and buried in mass graves like hundreds of others, or if he was arrested. Abu Kaed is my friend, and he is a peaceful man with no affiliation to any organization. Every day, I pray for his safety and for his quick return to us.

The occupation has committed thousands of crimes since its occupation of Palestine, practicing all forms of destruction, bombing, killing, and forced displacement against Palestinians. It continues building settlements in the West Bank. The occupation has violated all agreements and treaties, and has maintained a policy of killing Palestinians for over 76 years.

Even after the Oslo agreement in 1993 between the Palestinian Authority and the Israeli occupation authorities, the occupation continued its violations. This agreement was harmful to the Palestinian people. Arab and Islamic countries have intervened with many initiatives aimed at creating a Palestinian state and achieving permanent peace in the region. However, the occupation insists on continuing the killing, destruction, and displacement of Palestinians.

I miss my town of Julis, which is occupied. I miss our house and our land. I miss every detail of my childhood in occupied Palestine. I did not expect to reach the age of 91 with Palestine still occupied. The international community must intervene to find a permanent solution to the Palestinian issue. The occupation has likely killed over 40,000 Palestinians, injured over 75,000 in this war, and forced all the inhabitants of the Gaza Strip into tents.* The world must intervene and find a just solution to the Palestinian issue.

The policies of the occupation aimed at killing us and displacing us must stop. We are the indigenous people of the land, and we will never leave our land, no matter what happens. I hope this unjust war stops, and I can return to my occupied town of Julis before I die. This was my dream when I was a child, and it is still my dream as an elderly man. If I cannot live to see it fulfilled, my grandchildren will achieve it soon. ♦

---

* These estimates of Palestinians killed and injured by the Israeli military reflect the numbers as of May 2024, when this story was written. The numbers of Palestinians killed and injured in the genocide continue to rise.

Under Siege in Khan Younis

Manar Wadi

❝ The occupation forces called the center's official, Rawiya Hilles, and asked her to tell everyone in the center. They warned us to evacuate the place by 5 a.m., but there was no transportation available to take us to Rafah city. After extreme difficulty, my husband found a car, and we paid 600 shekels [160.50 USD] and a 50-kilogram [110-pound] bag of rice for the driver to take us to Rafah. ❞

AFTER the first week of the Israeli war on Gaza, I evacuated from my home in Jabalia refugee camp in the northern Gaza Strip. I suffered from the journey of displacement. I traveled from Nuseirat camp to Khan Younis city, then to Rafah city, then to Deir al-Balah city, and finally, I returned to Nuseirat camp. The hardest period of my displacement was during the occupation's raid on Nasser Hospital in Khan Younis, which forced us into a nearby building for a month. I saw death at every moment, and then fled from the heavy shelling. I don't know how I am still alive.

My name is Manar Wadi, and I am 30 years old. I am married to Mahmoud Wadi and I have three children: Ahmed, ten years old; Ayat, six years old; and Amir, one-and-a-half years old. We lived in Jabalia refugee camp in the northern Gaza Strip. After my marriage, I completed my university studies at Al-Quds Open University. I graduated in 2017 with a bachelor's degree in mathematics. I got a temporary job as a ninth-grade math teacher at Hamama School in the northern Gaza Strip. My goal was to help my husband and get a permanent job, but then the war came, destroying all our dreams.

After the Israeli shelling intensified in the northern Gaza Strip, my husband, my children, and I fled to Nuseirat camp in the center of the Strip. I lived in my cousin's house for a week. After heavy shelling in Nuseirat camp, my family and I headed to Khan Younis city in south Gaza.

We set up a tent in a vocational training center belonging to the Palestinian government, adjacent to Nasser Hospital in western Khan Younis. I felt the place was safe because it was near a hospital and because thousands of displaced people were living there. I bought wood, a tent, and blankets. I prepared my tent properly so that my family and I could live comfortably during the winter.

I bought 16 blankets, each costing 35 Israeli shekels [9.40 USD]. I thought I would live in the tent for a week or a month, but instead I lived in it for three months. This led me to buy large amounts of wood to reinforce the tent to withstand the rain. I also bought a gas cylinder for 500 shekels [133.80 USD], a gas cooker for 500 shekels, as well as dishes and kitchen utensils at prices ten times higher than before the war. My only concern was to provide everything necessary for my children.

After the end of the humanitarian ceasefire in November 2023, the Israeli forces stormed Khan Younis. My family and I thought the occupation wouldn't reach Nasser Hospital, where we were living as displaced people, as Khan Younis is a large city. We believed they would stay in the eastern areas of the city, so we decided to stay in our tent adjacent to the hospital, considering hospitals are protected under international humanitarian law.

A few days after the occupation stormed Khan Younis, we were surprised by the sounds of Israeli tanks. My husband tried to find the source of the noise, but Israeli drones fired at anyone who moved. I asked my husband not to go out, and we stayed in the tent encampment with thousands of other displaced people until the occupation forces approached us just a few meters away.

Israeli snipers occupied tall buildings around Nasser Hospital and prevented all displaced people from moving or leaving the tents. Israeli shelling continued fiercely around us until the occupation forces bombed the shelter center where we were living, resulting in the deaths of 13 people. The shelling caused a large fire at the site, which lasted from 12 noon until 10 p.m. My family managed to extinguish the fire with great difficulty.

We contacted the Red Cross to evacuate us. They instructed us to stay away from the center's gates and to remain inside the tents. The occupation forces threw tear gas grenades behind the center. My youngest son, Amir, who is a one-and-a-half-year-old, was affected by the gas and lost consciousness for more than ten hours. I carried him and ran through the shelling to Nasser Hospital, where he stayed for four days receiving treatment. Then, I returned to the shelter center with my husband and children.

The occupation forces called the center's official, Rawiya Hilles, and asked her to tell everyone in the center to evacuate the place by 5 a.m. There was no transportation available to take us to Rafah city. After extreme difficulty, my husband found a car, and we paid 600 shekels [160.50 USD] and a 50-kilogram [110-pound] bag of rice for the driver to take us to Rafah.

The car only had room for two people, so my husband and I sat with our children in our laps. We left nearly everything we owned in the tent. We could only take one tent, two mattresses, and some clothes for my children. We left behind all the food, drinks, clothes, and tools that I had bought in the school. My only thought was to save myself and my children from death.

Before successfully escaping the Israeli shelling, we tried many times to leave the center, raising white flags, but the Israeli snipers fired at us, and the occupation vehicles prevented us from leaving. We lived through the most difficult days of our lives, full of fear and death. We buried 13 displaced people, most of them children and women, who were killed by the Israeli shelling at the center. We buried them inside the center. By the grace of God, we survived, and we managed to reach Rafah after a month of the deadly Israeli siege.

My daughter, Ayat, suffered from seizures due to the continuous and intense Israeli shelling. Additionally, during the war, my infant son, Amir, experienced involuntary urination due to extreme fear. He also suffered from seizures after inhaling the Israeli tear gas. I am very afraid for my children, and there is no treatment available in Gaza.

After arriving in Rafah, we set up a tent in a displacement camp. The camp was frightening, filled with snake holes and harmful animals. We lived there for ten days, then we moved again to Deir al-Balah in the middle of the Gaza Strip. We lived there for three days in a tent next to my sister's house at the martyr Mohammed al-Dura stadium, then I returned to the Nuseirat camp. This time, I returned to a school-turned-shelter belonging to UNRWA in the middle of the camp.

I currently live with 12 other families in a small classroom. We've gotten to know each other during the war. I have now been living in the school for two months. The school was bombed by the Israelis twice, and dozens of displaced people were killed or injured. I try to keep my children with me all the time. I fear for them with the shelling that even shelter centers set up by international organizations are not safe from.

We suffer from poor distribution of food aid at the school. We only receive a box of canned goods every ten days. Sanitation and health conditions are very poor. The bathrooms are few and public, used by thousands. Water is scarce and causes many diseases. My children don't have enough clothes, and we don't have any money. All the money I had before the war has been spent. We are living in extremely catastrophic conditions.

My son needs prescription glasses, and we don't have money. There are no eye centers operating during the war. All I dream of now is for this war to end immediately, and for us to return to our home in Jabalia camp. I don't want to be displaced anywhere else. However, the shelling on the Nuseirat camp continues. The occupation forces stormed the camp less than a month ago, destroying dozens of houses and causing us extreme fear.

My dream before the war was to get a stable and permanent job to help my husband with household expenses. But now, we don't know anything about our home. We don't know whether it was destroyed or if it is still standing. I suffer from shortness of breath at the age of 30 due to inhaling smoke when cooking food over a fire. I hope to reunite with my husband and children in our home soon. I hope for Gaza to return to being a safe and beautiful place as it was before the war. We love life in peace and security, and we want Gaza to be safe forever. The war must stop immediately, and life must return to Gaza. ♦

Teaching 200 Children in Displacement Camps: How I Turn Displacement Tents into Schools

Ikram Talaat Ahmed

> I learned from the news that the Israeli forces had destroyed the Ibn Khaldoun Model School where I worked. During this oppressive war on the Gaza Strip, I've lost both of my jobs. Four teachers who used to work with me at the Noor Center have been killed. But I have not lost my love for work and my love for teaching children.

Before the war, I worked as an English language teacher at a kindergarten in the Gaza Strip. In the evenings, I gave private lessons to students at my own educational center beneath my house. I had been working since university, but during this war, I lost my job. My house and educational center were bombed, and the school where I worked was destroyed. I've lost everything in this war, but I've been able to turn my family's displacement tent into a small school for teaching displaced children.

My name is Ikram Talaat Ahmed. I am 29 years old. This is the story of our great loss caused by the Israeli occupation during their war on the Gaza Strip, and my resistance to the occupation through education.

I live with my family in the Bureij refugee camp in the middle of the Gaza Strip. Several years ago, I obtained a bachelor's degree in English language. I lived a happy, quiet life with my husband, Ramy Al-Batran, and my children, Celine, six years old, and Ibrahim, four years old. I got a job at the Ibn Khaldoun Model School, and also opened my own educational center in my house. I loved teaching very much; it's the noblest profession on earth. I spent most of my time teaching children until the war broke out. I've lost everything during these nearly eight tough months.

I worked as an English language teacher for children at the Ibn Khaldoun Model School kindergarten. I was very happy with my job. I love children and my profession very much. The greatest joy I've ever had in my life has been working in teaching and educating children.

After years of teaching, I managed to open my own educational center beneath my house in the Bureij refugee camp and named it the Noor Educational Center. I spent long hours giving private lessons to students from kindergarten to the preparatory stage. I was happy with the success of my private work and my ability to develop my educational project.

After the Israeli forces invaded the camps of the central governorate of the Gaza Strip, my family and I fled to the city of Deir

TEACHING 200 CHILDREN IN DISPLACEMENT CAMPS

al-Balah, where we set up a tent in the displacement camps. We have been living there since January 2024. Israeli forces invaded the Bureij camp for about a month, and after their withdrawal, my husband returned to check on our house, only to find it completely destroyed, along with my educational center.

I learned from the news that the Israeli forces had destroyed the Ibn Khaldoun Model School where I worked. During this oppressive war on the Gaza Strip, I've lost both of my jobs. Four teachers who used to work with me at the Noor Center have been killed. But I have not lost my love for work and my love for teaching children.

After spending about a month in the displacement tents in Deir al-Balah, and learning that the occupation had destroyed my house and educational center, I decided to resume teaching. My husband and I agreed to turn the tent we live in into a small school for teaching. The number of displaced students in the shelter camp is very large, and the students spend their time without benefit, as all aspects of life have been completely halted since the beginning of the war in the Gaza Strip.

My educational initiative began by teaching the children living near my tent. The idea was greatly accepted, admired, and encouraged by all the residents in the camp. I teach children from first grade to sixth grade. The number of students has reached over 200, and we receive new students every day who want to learn.

My educational tent initiative has now expanded, and three teachers volunteered to work with me in the tent. They are teacher Iman Basal, an English language teacher; teacher Hanin Al-Zareai, an Arabic language teacher; and teacher Dina Al-Zareai, a teacher for the preparatory stage, who supervises coordinating lessons at the educational tent.

I named the educational tent "Noor Educational Center" because I want the educational center that was destroyed by the occupation to continue, and I want our children to see the light and have a bright future. Palestinians continue their dedication to education in this harsh war. We try to revive the spirit of studying and education in the hearts and minds of our children despite the intense and continuous Israeli bombardment of the Gaza Strip for the past nearly eight months.

We face many challenges in teaching children at the educational tent. The biggest challenge is the narrow space of the tent, which is only three meters wide and seven meters long – not enough to accommodate the more than 200 students who spend several hours inside it every day for study and education.

We also face difficulty during daily lessons due to the high temperatures, the spread of insects, and the lack of necessary items such as pens, notebooks, and a whiteboard. Some students sit in the sand due to the lack of chairs and desks.

The students' enthusiasm for learning is very high. We started teaching the children of the displacement camp where we live, and then began teaching children from neighboring displacement camps. We in the Gaza Strip love education very much, and all parents care about educating their children, as the Gaza Strip is considered one of the most educated areas in the world.

My fellow teachers and I have noticed a significant decrease in the students' level of comprehension compared to before the Israeli war on the Gaza Strip. For the first few months, we found it difficult to establish students' academic foundations, such as reading simple words and pronouncing letters. Over time, there has been significant improvement in the students' comprehension levels. However, the difficult conditions of the war and the environment in which we live affect the students' mental abilities. This is the biggest obstacle in our work.

I dream of the war ending soon, and us returning to our normal lives before this war started. I hope to go back to my hobbies, like reading books. I wish for the Israeli massacres against us to stop, and for students to return to their schools. The war has caused all the students in Gaza to lose an entire academic year from their lives. We should now be preparing for end-of-year exams, but the war started at the beginning of the school year.

We are nearing the end of the academic year, yet the Israeli war on Gaza continues.

My big dreams are to rebuild my Noor Educational Center, to rebuild the Ibn Khaldoun School where I worked for several years, and to reopen all the schools. I hope that the Palestinian Ministry of Education will find a way to compensate the students for this academic year, and that we can find a way to save their academic year so that they do not lose it completely. But this requires an immediate cessation of the war and finding alternative shelter centers for the over 1.5 million displaced people across the Gaza Strip who are currently crowded into schools.

I have fulfilled my duty toward my Palestinian people. I am a teacher, and it is my duty to educate children and ensure the emergence of an educated, cultured generation capable of uplifting our homeland. I continued my work during the war with courage, and I ensured that Gaza remains, as everyone knows it, a hub for knowledge and scholars. The occupation has destroyed dozens of schools and universities during its war. All the remaining schools have been turned into shelter centers. The schools will need significant rehabilitation to be available for teaching students again after the war ends. Our students also need extensive psychological rehabilitation to overcome the significant and dangerous effects of the war they are suffering from.

We need everyone's cooperation and the convergence of all energies and capabilities to save the academic year. I hope that my educational tent initiative can be supported and receive stationery and basic school supplies. My dream is for the war to end soon, and for us to return to teaching our children in schools and educational centers that are suitable for them – designed for children's education with the familiar academic atmosphere our students were used to before the war. Teachers are messengers of knowledge and education. We continue our educational mission despite all the great risks surrounding us, with confidence that the war will end and the educational success in the Gaza Strip will continue. ♦

Today, I Sell Chips, but Tomorrow, I Will Be a Doctor

Aseel Al Hawajri

> ❝ My name is Aseel Al Hawajri, I am a 14-year-old student from Juhar Al-Dik in Gaza, selling chips and sweets to provide my family with money to get by. Today we are displaced, but tomorrow the war will stop, and we will return to rebuild our homes. I will continue studying until I achieve my dream. ❞

THE Israeli occupation transformed me from a distinguished university student to a salesperson, selling chips in a small stall. Every day, I wake up early in the morning to help my mother prepare chips and sweets. Then, I put them on a tray and go to the schoolyard. I sit there all day until I sell everything we prepared. The cold was biting in the winter, and now the sun's heat is intense, but I am determined to help my family and save some money for them.

I used to live with my family in Wadi Gaza village, also known as Juhar Al-Dik village, northeast of the central governorate of Gaza. My father obtained an apartment in Tika Towers from the Ministry of Social Development several years ago. This was our home until we evacuated to an UNRWA school in Nuseirat camp on the first day of the war, where we have been living now for more than seven months.

Before the war, all of us who lived in Tika Towers were from the poorer segments of Gaza. The Palestinian government granted us these residential apartments, which are overseen by Turkey, several years ago. Before moving to Tika Towers, none of us residents had owned houses – we lived in small rooms or rented apartments. Before our move, my family had been living in an apartment east of the Juhar Al-Dik area.

I lived half of my life in rented apartments and the other half in our apartment in Tika Towers. The apartment we obtained from the government was small, but we loved it. It was the first home we lived in securely, without my father having to pay for our housing. Our home symbolized everything beautiful in our lives.

During the first days of Israel's war, my family, the residents of Tika Towers, and the residents of Juhar Al-Dik moved to UNRWA shelters, as we lived very close to the eastern border of the Gaza Strip. The occupation targeted the area with dozens of rockets, forcing us to flee in search of safety.

We spent the first month of the war in shelters. We returned home during the first truce at the end of last November to check on our house in Juhar Al-Dik. We found great destruction in the area, and after the truce, which lasted for seven days, the occupation bombed Tika Towers, Hamad Towers, and Kuwaiti Towers. The occupation destroyed all residential towers in the Juhar Al-Dik area, depriving thousands of families of housing.

All of these families, including mine, did not own a house before obtaining residential apartments in the Juhar Al-Dik area. Now, thousands of families have returned to their original suffering. The occupation has destroyed their homes and apartments, taking away the greatest joy in our lives.

The occupation also bombed the school-turned-shelter we lived in twice during the war, killing and injuring many displaced people. The first time the occupation bombed the school, I was playing volleyball in the schoolyard and narrowly escaped the bombing. Many were injured. The second time, a few days ago, I was selling food at my small stall, and only God saved me. Even the school-turned-shelter we evacuated to is being bombed by the occupation. We don't feel safe here.

I am very afraid of the bombings and the sound of the rockets. When I hear bombing, I grab the chip tray and run into my mother's classroom. We live in a classroom with ten other families. My sister and I sleep on one mattress. We don't have food every day, and finding water is very difficult. We cook by lighting fires, and my father spends all day searching for firewood to prepare meals. I earn very little from selling food, but it helps us during these difficult days. Our lives have been painful and harsh since the first day of the Israeli war on Gaza.

I am a student at Wafa Al Amer School in the area of Juhar Al-Dik. I study in the second preparatory grade. I am one of the best students, thank God. I've received certificates of appreciation at the end of each year for my excellence in all subjects, and I am honored by the school administration for my high grades.

Before the war, my father, who is 41 years old, worked as a craftsman in tiling. Work was not always available in Gaza due to the difficult financial circumstances of the people because of the 17-year Israeli blockade imposed on the Strip. The blockade began four years before my birth. My family suffered financially because of the blockade, and now they suffer even more due to the war.

Before the war, my father made sure to provide me with all the school supplies and necessities I would need. I studied in a school affiliated with the Palestinian government, not an UNRWA school, due to the distance between my residential area and UNRWA schools. My parents always encouraged me to study and strive to excel in all subjects. I studied hard to bring them the happiness they desire.

My school, Wafa Al Amer, was not spared from the Israeli occupation's bombing. The occupation aircraft bombed the school and destroyed it. The occupation not only destroyed our homes, but also bombed the school where I had memories of my first steps in education. The occupation has deprived us of housing and our right to education. I loved my school very much, and I loved my teachers and classmates. I have beautiful memories there because I was well known for my academic distinction. But the occupation destroyed everything that brought us joy.

Ever since I was young, I have dreamed of becoming a skilled doctor. I have worked hard in my studies since the first grade to achieve this ambition. I wanted to have a high and distinguished GPA for when I reach the stage of general secondary education. I want my GPA to qualify me for a scholarship to study medicine, as my father's circumstances do not allow him to afford the university fees. This is why I study and strive to achieve this dream. This is my primary goal in life.

But the occupation bombed my school and destroyed it. I have been living in a shelter since the beginning of the war. Today, everyone sees me as a chip and homemade sweets seller at the shelter. People do not know that I am one of the highest achieving students in my studies, and that I have big ambitions, which I will achieve soon.

Today, people see the 14-year-old girl, Aseel, as a chip seller in the shelter, but tomorrow they will see Dr. Aseel, who refused to surrender, challenged all obstacles, continued studying, worked hard, and achieved her dream. Today we are displaced, but tomorrow the war will stop, and we will return to rebuild our homes. I will continue studying until I achieve my dream.

I am happy that I can help my family with their expenses during this war. My parents dedicated their lives to me and my siblings.

Today, I stand by them and help them overcome these circumstances. Soon, I will be able to achieve my dream and theirs, and they will all be proud of me. This war will not be able to kill my dreams or prevent me from achieving them.

My little sister, Rital, helps me sell food every day. Rital dreams of becoming an engineer and rebuilding what the occupation destroyed during this war. My dream is to become a doctor and help my people with their medical needs, as the occupation has killed and injured tens of thousands during this war.

I've lost many relatives and know many who've been wounded during this war. I've lost all the members of my aunt's family. I've lost many of my classmates. The occupation has separated me from my classmates, relatives, and neighbors. I hope the war ends, we return to Juhar Al-Dik soon, and our house is rebuilt quickly. I am ready to live in a tent to continue my education, even at a school made of tents. I am ready to do anything to achieve my dream and make my parents and family proud of me. The war now stands between me and achieving my dreams. I hope it ends soon so we can return to diligence and hard work to achieve our goals in life. ♦

Widowed on the Fifth Day of the War

Fidaa Al-Shakhreet

> We thought living in tents would be safe, believing that the Israeli shelling would be confined to areas designated by the occupation forces. We flee based on their instructions. But wherever we go, we are pursued by shelling. Death stalks us around the clock. The shelling is everywhere, and fear has accompanied us since the first day of the war.

My husband was martyred on the fifth day of the war. I used to live with my husband and our three children in a simple house in Beit Hanoun, the northernmost part of the Gaza Strip. Life before the war was difficult, but we were happy to be together. We evacuated on the first day of the war as our house was close to the border with the 1948 lands. The occupation killed my husband on the fifth day of the war, leaving me with the responsibility of raising three children alone.

I married Saeed Muayyin Al-Shakhreet seven years ago. Allah blessed us with three children: Zainab, six years old; Abdullah, four years old; and the youngest, Razan, who is only one year old.

Our house was near the Erez Israeli military checkpoint. Our journey of suffering began on the first day of the war and has continued for almost eight consecutive months.

When the Israeli war on Gaza began on October 7, 2023, my family and I fled to UNRWA schools in Beit Hanoun. As the bombing intensified, we moved to other schools-turned-shelters in Jabalia camp. After my husband was martyred, we stayed in Jabalia camp for a week longer. Our suffering intensified after my husband's martyrdom.

I stayed with my children in the Jabalia camp schools for a week. As Israeli airstrikes intensified, we fled to Nuseirat camp in the central Gaza Strip. The 30-kilometer [18.6-mile] journey of displacement was exhausting. Having lost my husband, I was alone with my children. There is no one to help us in this fierce war.

We lived in tents at Mumdhuh Saeedam School in Nuseirat camp for more than two months until, in the beginning of January, the occupation forces issued evacuation notices. I took my children to Deir al-Balah city, searching for a place to live in schools, but found none. We slept in the open air for several days, enduring severe cold. My children fell ill during this period.

Residents of Deir al-Balah helped me set up a tent for me and my children. We've now been living in this tent for five consecutive months in a camp for displaced people in the Al-Bassa area west of Deir al-Balah city. Conditions are extremely difficult; we lack the bare necessities of life – food, water, and daily needs. Life in the tents is painful and harsh, and we have never gotten used to it. Harmful insects fill the tents. During winter, we endured severe

WIDOWED ON THE FIFTH DAY OF THE WAR

cold. Water fills our tents during the rain. Now, we suffer from extreme heat and high humidity inside the tents.

On the fifth day of the Israeli war on Gaza, October 11, 2023, my husband went to inspect our house in Beit Hanoun city. I asked him not to go because the Israeli bombing was heavy. We were living in schools-turned-shelters in Jabalia camp without clothes, food, or water.

My husband went to our house with his uncle and brother to bring us necessities. They risked their lives to provide for us, even in that difficult situation.

My husband, his uncle, and his brother entered our house, and the occupation forces bombed it, destroying it. They were martyred instantly, and many of our relatives are still missing under the rubble of our destroyed houses in Beit Hanoun city. My husband, his uncle, and his brother were buried in the cemeteries of Jabalia camp, far away from our houses and Beit Hanoun's cemetery, where we used to bury our relatives.

I couldn't comprehend that my husband had become a martyr and that I would live the rest of my life as a widow, now responsible for raising three children alone. This news was shocking and painful. My husband, Saeed, was a man whom I loved and who loved me. We lived together for seven years, during which we formed our small family – I don't know how I will continue my life without him.

Our displacement journey for nearly eight months has only added to my suffering. I have become both a mother and a father to my children.

Life inside the tents is extremely difficult. We have no water, and the temperatures are unbearably high. There are no places for our children to play, and the area lacks cleanliness. We have no lighting at night and sleep in complete darkness. We try to finish all our tasks before darkness falls. We have been living in tents for almost eight months, but we have never adapted to tent life.

We suffer from many harmful insects and other animals in and around the tents, including scorpions, snakes, flies, and mosquitoes. We experience influenza, allergies, and colds due to fluctuating temperatures, with extreme heat during the day and cold at night. We have no water to maintain our hygiene or the personal hygiene of our children. The situation is difficult in every way.

We rely on fire to prepare food. We cook canned food obtained from UNRWA. We receive a small food basket every week to ten days. I feed my children small pieces of candy to pacify them until I can prepare a meal. We eat only one meal a day, either breakfast or lunch. We do not have enough food for two or three meals a day as we did before the war. We try to survive with what little food we have.

Out of necessity, I sell canned goods to have some money to buy food for my children. I go out daily in search of work but cannot find any. I walk several kilometers daily searching for firewood to cook food and sometimes manage to find a little, but mostly I don't. All displaced people search for wood and endure the same suffering, but I am now a mother and father. There is no one to help me, no one to stand by my side. I lost my support and my husband on the fifth day of the war.

We thought living in tents would be safe, believing that the Israeli shelling would be confined to areas designated by the occupation forces. We flee based on their instructions. But wherever we go, we are pursued by shelling. Death stalks us around the clock. The shelling is everywhere, and fear has accompanied us since the first day of the war.

A mosque adjacent to the displaced people's camp where we live in Deir al-Balah city, was bombed. Rocket shrapnel and rubble fell on our tents, injuring my neighbors and significantly damaging our tent. My children and I survived the Israeli bombing.

I do not feel safe anywhere in the Gaza Strip. There is no safety for me and my children. Every day, we are exposed to heavy shelling near the displacement tents. Fear for my children's safety accompanies me constantly. Everything around us reminds us that we are exposed to death at all times.

If we do not die from Israeli missiles, death threatens us with scorpion stings, snake bites, or the diseases we suffer from in this miserable life. Death stalks us at all times. I try to protect my children and keep them safe. They are my husband's trust to me, but what is happening in Gaza during this war is beyond my capabilities. This war is very harsh, and we have never seen anything like it before.

On the first day of our marriage, my husband and I agreed to work hard to provide a decent life for our children. But today, my husband has become a martyr; the occupation killed him and destroyed our house completely. We have been living in tents for nearly eight months, but my dream of providing a decent life for my children is still alive. I will work hard to preserve the trust of my martyr husband.

I dream of completing my children's education and providing them with a decent life. I dream of them living a safe life away from risks. I am now solely responsible for them, which is a great responsibility for a young woman. I have turned from a bride into a mother without a husband, but I will protect my children. I hope that the war will end soon, that I will be able to rebuild my house, and that the daily killing we are experiencing in this war will stop. I would be ready to live in a tent on my destroyed house. The day I return to my house and the day I visit my husband's grave will be the best days of my life. ◆

Israel Killed My Daughter on Her Third Birthday

Tareq Fareed Al Hajj

> **❝** I spoke to them, but they didn't respond. I quickly took them to the hospital, praying to God all the way that they would be alive, but when I arrived at Al-Aqsa Hospital, the doctors informed me that they had been martyred due to the bombing. **❞**

My name is Tareq Fareed Al Hajj. I am 30 years old. It happened on Tuesday, March 19, 2024, the birthday of my little daughter Suwar, who turned three years old. I had promised her that her birthday would be special, but on her third birthday, the occupation killed her.

That day, my mother had asked me to let Suwar sleep at my

brother Abdullah's house because the occupation had bombed my neighbor's house, destroying it. My mother had been staying with my brother since the first month of the war. My wife refused to let our children sleep there, saying she was afraid for our daughters and couldn't sleep without them. But she promised to visit my mother in the morning with Suwar and Amar.

In the early days of the Israeli war on the Gaza Strip, the occupation bombed a house near us, resulting in the death of five-year-old Suleiman Yasser Al Hajj, Amar's friend from kindergarten. She used to play with him all the time, and constantly talked to her mother about him. She was deeply saddened by his martyrdom, and entered a difficult psychological state for several days. The martyrdom of Suleiman wasn't the only reason for Amar's distress. The sounds of intense and continuous Israeli bombing caused fear, sleeplessness, and constant crying among my daughters. Fear gripped all of us, adults and children alike, in the Gaza Strip.

Before their deaths, my wife and I tried to calm our daughters, telling them that Suleiman was in paradise and had gone to a better place. But Amar remained sad; she wanted to play with Suleiman and go to kindergarten with him, but Suleiman was gone forever, separated from us by Israeli rockets.

We lived in an apartment in Tika Towers in the Juhar Al-Dik area in the central governorate, but the occupation bombed all the residential towers there, and I lost my home, my safe haven. This forced me to find an apartment close to my family's home in Nuseirat camp, which I have rented since the war's early days.

My daughters experienced displacement and death. After the occupation invaded the camps in central Gaza, my family and I fled to a relative's home in Rafah, in the south of the Gaza Strip. The house was crowded with displaced people. Rafah's population exceeded 1.5 million due to the influx of displaced people, while its population before the war was no more than 250,000 Palestinians. My wife only managed to get two mattresses, so she and our daughters slept on them, while I slept on the street with my relatives. Despite the crowded conditions, I chose to flee to Rafah to ensure my family's safety, preferring to sleep in the street rather than risk their lives.

After repeated Israeli airstrikes on our neighborhood, my family and I fled to my parents' house. However, a few days later, the occupation bombed a house adjacent to my parents' home, causing complete destruction. My father, mother, and everyone in the house were injured. After receiving treatment at the hospital, everyone moved to my brother Abdullah's small apartment, which consisted of only three rooms. The occupation forces stormed the eastern outskirts of Nuseirat camp, causing our family to scatter. My wife, daughters, and I fled to Rafah with my parents and some siblings. My brother Abdullah and his family fled to Deir al-Balah. The occupation forces eventually withdrew, but living in tents was extremely difficult, with diseases, epidemics, and hunger spreading among everyone.

Before the humanitarian ceasefire in November 2023, the occupation bombed the neighborhood where my small grocery store was, destroying everything. My brother Abdullah, my father, and I lost our livelihoods. My parents and siblings used to call me daily and talk to my daughters. My children were my parents' first grandchildren, and everyone loved them. Since the beginning of the war, we've tried to assure my parents of our safety, despite our fears of being bombed. The last call I received was on Sunday evening from my mother and brother, who congratulated us on Suwar's third birthday. They asked me to stay home and take care of my family, and I promised them I would.

I didn't expect our apartment to be targeted because it's in a civilian area, and all the residents are peaceful and have no connection to any Palestinian organization. Our apartment had four rooms. We chose to sleep in the two rooms on the northeast side, away from the street and adjacent to the home of the Habbash family, all of whom are peaceful civilians.

In the house, we stayed with my cousin and his wife, who were displaced after their house was bombed. They joined us for Suwar's

ISRAEL KILLED MY DAUGHTER ON HER THIRD BIRTHDAY

birthday party, and we all went to sleep. Our night ended early when the occupation bombed the Habbash family's house at exactly 9 p.m. I awoke to find a concrete column on my wife, and stones covering both my body and hers. I was on the edge of the first-floor apartment, and I lifted the rubble off myself and began searching for my daughters.

I searched for my daughters for a long time, lifting rubble and stones with my hands. I was injured and couldn't see well. After an hour of searching, the neighbors told me that my daughters had been taken to the hospital. My wife and I were then taken to the hospital by ambulance, but when we arrived, we didn't find our daughters. I searched the children's section but couldn't find them, so we returned home to search for them again.

We searched for Amar and Suwar but couldn't find them. After a long search, we found them far from the house. The occupation's rockets had thrown them onto the street due to the intensity of the bombing, and they were martyred instantly. I spoke to them, but they didn't respond. I quickly took them to the hospital, praying to God all the way that they would be alive, but when I arrived at Al-Aqsa Hospital, the doctors informed me that they had been martyred due to the bombing.

My two daughters were martyred, and my wife was injured with two fractures in her spine, nerve damage in her hands, and fractures and bruises all over her body. My eyes, face, and back were all injured, and I had bruises all over my body. A piece of shrapnel lodged in my skull. The bombing took place at night, and no one could be buried due to the dangerous situation and the intensified bombing. So, we wrapped my daughters' bodies, and I placed them near the morgue's refrigerator because there was no room left for more martyrs. The Israeli bombing of the residential neighborhood resulted in about 25 martyrs and wounded dozens of other people. The hospital was filled with martyrs, most of whom were women and children.

The next morning, my daughters' aunts came to the hospital to bid them farewell. After seeing them, they screamed, "Suwar and Amar, cover them from the cold." My brother Abdullah, who was present, brought a blanket and covered them. Everyone loved them very much. They had done nothing wrong to deserve being killed by the occupation.

I dreamed of educating my daughters and fulfilling all their dreams. Amar wanted to become an engineer and Suwar wanted to become a dentist. But now, the occupation killed their dreams and took my daughters from me. I will not forgive the occupation or anyone who caused their deaths and deprived me of them.

My daughters Amar and Suwar were covered with a blanket to keep them from getting cold. Then my wife, their mother, and I bid them farewell from our hospital beds. The doctors treated our wounds, but the wounds in our hearts have no cure. My family buried them in the cemetery, but there wasn't enough space, so they were buried in one grave above my grandfather Hassan, who passed away many years ago. Amar and Suwar were sisters and friends, and now they are martyrs, their blood a testament to the crimes of the occupation against the children of Gaza. My wife and I are still receiving treatment and hoping to rebuild our family. We live in regret for losing our two flowers, Amar and Suwar. We won't be able to see them or celebrate their birthdays anymore. Their lives were stopped at only ages five and three. ♦

Creating Joy Despite Displacement
Akram Abdul Nabi Al-Ajrami

> The occupation threatens to raid the city of Deir al-Balah as it raided Rafah a week ago. We do not want to evacuate again; we want to return to our homes and live on the ruins of our destroyed houses. We do not want to live in these tents that remind us of the worst days of our lives. . . .We haven't felt settled anywhere we've been displaced to. We've been exhausted from moving between cities and camps in the central and southern Gaza Strip.

I SPEND my time organizing recreational and educational activities for children and all of the other residents in the tents. We have been living in tents for several months, and there is no source of entertainment for our children. These days are the worst of our lives, especially for our children. We suffer greatly living in these conditions. I work hard to organize activities that alleviate the suffering of our children and bring some joy and happiness to their hearts. My name is Akram Abdul Nabi Al-Ajrami. I am 61 years old. This is my daily life as a displaced person living in a tent in the city of Deir al-Balah, in the central Gaza Strip.

As an elderly man, the occupation forces did not spare me for my old age, nor did they spare our children, women, elders, or youth. The bombing we are subjected to in the Gaza Strip is unprecedented. If a major country were subjected to this bombing, it would have ended in the first week. However, our love for our homeland Palestine, our insistence on our land, and our refusal to emigrate from it have pushed us to stand firm. If the resistance defends us with some simple weapons, we must also resist the occupation by standing firm on our land and refusing to emigrate, no matter what happens. We live in catastrophic conditions, but we are the owners of this land; we are its people, and we will never leave it.

During the first days of the war on the Gaza Strip, I fled from the Jabalia camp in the north, where my house is located and where I lived with my sons and grandchildren, to Nuseirat camp in the middle of the Gaza Strip, where I stayed for a month. After the bombing intensified on the camp, we left to find a safer place.

The occupation asked us to evacuate to areas south of the Gaza Valley, and we thought that Nuseirat camp was safer than Jabalia camp because it is in the south of the Gaza Strip. But bombing and destruction reached all areas of the camp, which forced us to leave Nuseirat and search for a safer place.

Our displacement journey after Nuseirat camp was even harsher and more bitter. We fled to the city of Rafah in the south of the Gaza Strip, and stayed there in tents for displaced people for nearly two months. The crowding was severe and food aid was scarce. We spent many days without food; our children slept without eating. Their crying pained me and made me feel helpless all the time.

After Rafah, we returned again to Nuseirat camp for three weeks. Then, the occupation raided the camps in the middle of the Strip, and we evacuated to tents in the city of Deir al-Balah. We have been living in these tents for a month and a half.

My family and I suffered greatly on the way from Jabalia to Deir al-Balah; we lost a lot of money and walked tens of kilometers on foot. I do not want to repeat this experience again. We have experienced enough suffering, fatigue, and torment. I want to return from this tent to my house in the Jabalia camp. The occupation threatens to raid the city of Deir al-Balah as it raided Rafah a week ago. We do not want to evacuate again; we want to return to our homes and live on the ruins of our destroyed houses. We do not want to live in these tents that remind us of the worst days of our lives.

We haven't felt settled anywhere we've been displaced to. We've been exhausted from moving between cities and camps in the central and southern Gaza Strip. Our children have also suffered; they've shared every aspect of the hardship and displacement we've experienced moment by moment. They too lived in tents and endured cold, rain, heat, diseases, and insect bites. Shrapnel from bombings hit several houses adjacent to our tents. There is no safe place in Gaza.

After the exhausting journey of displacement we've endured for several months, I decided to organize some uplifting activities for the displaced. I have a beautiful voice, but being an elderly man, I'm not capable of organizing activities that require movement and play. So, I organized activities for residents to recite *salawat*, praises of the Prophet Muhammad (peace be upon him), in my tent and neighboring tents. Our displaced neighbors invited me to organize activities in their tents, and they were delighted with the praise of the Prophet, as it's one of the religious customs beloved by the people of Gaza. We usually organize such activities on various religious occasions. However, the prolonged duration of the war has deprived us of them.

The war started a month after the beginning of the academic year in the Gaza Strip, and it's been ongoing for over seven months now. We're on the verge of the end of the school year, but Gaza's students have lost this year. The occupation deprived them of education, just as it deprived them of their right to live in security and peace like the rest of the world.

After settling into the city of Deir al-Balah for over a month and a half, one of the displaced teachers from a neighboring tent approached us and asked for a tent to be designated for teaching children, to compensate them slightly for the complete loss of their academic year.

We were very happy with this initiative from the displaced teacher, and I immediately allocated my tent during certain hours of the day for use in teaching the displaced children. Every day, children gather in my tent to receive the education that was denied to them by the occupation. This is useful time amid the intense bombing of all governorates in the Strip.

The education tent is important for us; it's beneficial for our children and provides them with some knowledge that the occupation has deprived them of. This educational activity is crucial for us and for the future of our children. We will work to make it successful and look for other activities to support our children and alleviate the difficult circumstances they're experiencing because of this war.

I used to own a beautiful house in the Jabalia camp in the northern Gaza Strip. My house consisted of several floors, where I lived with my sons and grandchildren. We left it in search of safety after the occupation invaded the north and dozens of neighboring houses were bombed. My beautiful house was destroyed.

I learned from my neighbors in the Jabalia camp that my house was destroyed, and that the occupation demolished all the houses around it. I was deeply saddened by the loss of my house, as it took great effort over many years to build it. It holds beautiful memories for us; it's where my sons established their families, where my grandchildren were first embraced, and where I experienced my youth and old age. I dream that the war will end soon, that the suffering we're enduring will end urgently, and that these difficult days will end, so we can return to our homes, safely, very soon.

I've lost many relatives, neighbors, and friends who've become martyrs in this war. We've lost our homes to the occupation's destruction. The occupation forced us to live for several months in conditions we're not accustomed to. We owned beautiful houses – we have never been accustomed to living in tents.

We all realize that with patience and steadfastness on our land, these difficult days will pass, and we will return to our homes soon, victorious. The occupation has been killing us since the beginning of the occupation of Palestine, and all international organizations are watching what we're going through. This pain must end immediately.

This war has caused pain to all the residents of the Gaza Strip. Every house contains a martyr, a wounded person, or a prisoner. Every family has been targeted by the bombing of their house or neighbors' homes. Every house in the Gaza Strip has been affected by the bombing; they have targeted every place in the Strip.

All the people of Gaza suffer from hunger and lack of food and water. All the people of Gaza suffer from the shortage of medicine and the collapse of the health system. We hope that the war will end soon, and that all these difficult conditions we're experiencing will end. I hope to return to the Jabalia camp as soon as possible. I miss my home and the neighborhood I live in. I miss meeting my neighbors and relatives. I miss my life before the war. ◆

Providing Medical Services Under Impossible Conditions

Ahmed Nasr Halas

> ❝ I hope the world looks at us with humanity and stops this war. They should provide medicine and medical equipment to the people of the Gaza Strip. I am doing my duty to the best of my ability during this harsh war, and it is the duty of the international community to stop the war, rebuild the Gaza Strip, and hold the occupation accountable for its unlimited crimes against all of the people of Gaza. ❞

DURING the intense Israeli war on the Gaza Strip, the occupation destroyed the two pharmacies I owned in Gaza City; I lost my job and sole source of income. Despite this, I felt a responsibility to serve the displaced people of my nation.

MEDICAL SERVICES UNDER IMPOSSIBLE CONDITIONS

I opened a small pharmacy in the tent where I now live, having been displaced myself. I work around the clock to provide medical services and medications to thousands of displaced people, finding great happiness in alleviating their suffering. This is my situation and the situation of hundreds of thousands of displaced people who have lost most medical services during the Israeli war on the Gaza Strip. My name is Ahmed Nasr Halas, and I am 42 years old.

I studied pharmacy in Ukraine at Zaporizhzhia State Medical University, graduating in 2007. Then I returned to Palestine, my homeland, where I lived with my family in the Shuja'iyya neighborhood, east of Gaza City. I got married, and God blessed me with eight children. I lived a happy life with them.

At the beginning of my career, I worked as a pharmacist in several private pharmacies in the Gaza Strip. My first dream as a pharmacist was to open my own pharmacy. I worked hard to make this a reality, and in 2010, I opened my own pharmacy on Green Market Street in the Shuja'iyya neighborhood and named it "Ahmed Pharm 1." I provided medical services to residents during the Israeli war on Gaza in 2012, the 2014 war, and during all the other rounds of aggression waged by the occupation on Gaza before this war.

I continued to work in my pharmacy, gaining experience, and getting to know the hundreds of patients who visited my pharmacy constantly. I earned people's trust, which encouraged me to open a second pharmacy in 2014, also in the Shuja'iyya neighborhood, near Abu Maher Halas Square. I named it "Ahmed Pharm 2." My happiness was immense, and I spent all my time serving my patients and providing them with medical services.

I come from a well-known family in Gaza City, which added to peoples' confidence in my services. I provided most of the medications needed by patients, developed my business, and provided job opportunities for four of my colleagues in the two pharmacies I owned. From the beginning, my dream was their dream. We worked together, succeeded together, and shared everything together. I had bigger dreams too, like opening my own pharmaceutical company, completing my master's and doctoral degrees in my specialization, and opening more pharmacies in different areas of the Gaza Strip to provide services to citizens and develop my business.

At the beginning of the Israeli war on the Gaza Strip in October 2023, I continued to work in my pharmacies, providing medical services to all the patients in Shuja'iyya neighborhood. However, during the early days of the war, the occupation bombed a nearby mosque, Al-Islah Mosque, which completely destroyed my second pharmacy. Like most Gaza City residents, I fled with my family.

The journey of displacement was harsh and bitter. I spent two weeks in the Nuseirat camp in the middle of the Gaza Strip. The occupation bombed the building we had taken refuge in, so I moved with my family to the village of Al-Zawayda for a month. After the occupation bombed the area surrounding where we were living, I moved again with my family to the city of Rafah, where we stayed for a month. Due to severe overcrowding, we moved to Deir al-Balah in the middle of the Gaza Strip.

My remaining friends in Shuja'iyya told me that the occupation had destroyed my first pharmacy during the third month of the war when they invaded Gaza City. Thus, the occupation destroyed the dream I had worked so hard to achieve, the dream I spent many sleepless nights working toward.

I lost my home when the occupation bombed Shuja'iyya. The occupation deprived me of my home and my job, and my four colleagues lost their jobs as well. Since the beginning of the war, we have been jobless, living in tents under catastrophic health conditions. We lack all the essentials of life – we have no treatment, no medicine, no water, and no food. In addition to the continuous Israeli bombing across all the provinces of the Gaza Strip, we feel unsafe in every area, as the occupation has turned the Gaza Strip into a major battlefield.

I got the idea of opening a pharmacy in the tent where I live, considering the tens of thousands of displaced people in the city of Deir al-Balah. I live in a tent for displaced people directly on

MEDICAL SERVICES UNDER IMPOSSIBLE CONDITIONS | 121

the seafront street. There are no pharmacies in the displacement camp, and the pharmacies that are still operating are far from the displaced people's tents. It's very risky for people to try to get medicine from pharmacies in the center of Deir al-Balah, especially when the Israeli bombing intensifies at night.

I thought about how I could alleviate the suffering of the displaced people in the city of Deir al-Balah. So, I decided to open a pharmacy in the tent I live in, and I put up a small sign across the tent that read "Ahmed Pharm." I made some shelves from wood, and I covered my tent with nylon to protect it from the rain. I bought some medicines and started my work in the tent. There was a large turnout of displaced people at my pharmacy. Initially, I felt a bit embarrassed, but after hearing encouraging words from the people and seeing the happiness on the faces of my patients, I decided to continue my work at the pharmacy in my tent. I provide urgent medications needed by the displaced, and continue to work there late into the night.

I face significant difficulties in providing medications because many pharmaceutical companies in the Gaza Strip have been destroyed. The remaining few are closed and have not been operational since the beginning of the war. Additionally, the occupation has destroyed much of the healthcare system in the Gaza Strip, shutting down many hospitals and health centers completely, depriving over two million Palestinians of their right to treatment and access to medication.

I walk long distances, but in the end, I've only been able to find painkillers, antibiotics, gastrointestinal medications, and some other basic supplies needed by the displaced. I wish I could offer more services and medications to the displaced, but the current circumstances prevent me from doing so. I lack the funds to purchase more medications, and I don't have transportation to visit pharmacies that are still operational in Rafah. Additionally, some medications require refrigeration, and we lack electricity and solar power devices to operate the refrigerators. The quantity of medications is very limited, and many diseases have spread among the displaced due to water shortages and the occupation's bombing of sewage networks.

I go out to displaced people's tents every night to provide them with some injections and medications they need. This requires great effort from me, but I am happy to serve the displaced and alleviate their suffering. I feel a great sense of joy when I relieve people's pain and provide them with the necessary medications. All those living in tents have been deprived of their homes by the occupation and forced into a new life they are not accustomed to and cannot adapt to.

I dream that the war will stop immediately and that I will soon be able to rebuild my two pharmacies and resume their operations to serve my family, neighbors, and all patients in the Shuja'iyya neighborhood. It is true that the occupation destroyed the pharmacies I worked hard to open, but my dream is still alive. I still dream of opening a pharmaceutical company and completing my master's and doctoral studies.

I hope the world looks at us with humanity and stops this war. They should provide medicine and medical equipment to the people of the Gaza Strip. I am doing my duty to the best of my ability during this harsh war, and it is the duty of the international community to stop the war, rebuild the Gaza Strip, and hold the occupation accountable for its unlimited crimes against all of the people of Gaza. The occupation has destroyed our lives, ruined everything we have, and made us live in tents for more than seven months. However, we are determined to continue our dream and rebuild Gaza, which we love, were born in, and will not abandon. We will continue to develop Gaza to provide a suitable life for our children. ♦

Raising My Martyred Son's Children

Nasreen Naeem Al-Hilu

❝ We live in shelters under difficult living conditions, without any money. The children need food and drink, and we struggle to provide even a little. There is no work in Gaza, and we have no means to sustain ourselves. ❞

My story begins on the first day of the Israeli war on the Gaza Strip. My name is Nasreen Naeem Al-Hilu, and I am 47 years old, from Gaza City. I have been living in tents for displaced people since the second day of the war. Occupation forces bombed our neighbor's house, destroying their home and my family's home along with it.

The residents of our neighborhood evacuated the area. I went to my son Haitham Ziad Al-Hilu's house, located in the Sabra neighborhood south of Gaza City. We stayed there for a month, but as the bombing intensified, we fled. The house was completely bombed, and my son Mohammed, 27 years old, was martyred. He was extracted with great difficulty from under the rubble.

The occupation forces intensified their indiscriminate bombing of Gaza City, targeting residential neighborhoods and destroying them. After the bombing of my son Haitham's house and the martyrdom of my son Mohammed, we decided to flee to the southern valley areas, which the occupation forces declared as safe zones. We headed to Khan Younis.

We walked on foot, accompanied by children, women, and elderly people, for several kilometers. The occupation forces had divided the Gaza Strip into two parts, and designated Salah al-Din Street as the street for civilians to use to exit. We walked amid tanks, shelling, and heavy gunfire until we reached Sheikh Jabr School in Khan Younis, in the south of the Gaza Strip. The school was filled with thousands of displaced people seeking safety from the Israeli bombing.

We stayed at Sheikh Jabr School for three months. The school administration provided us with one meal a day, and we struggled greatly to provide bread and food for our children. My children and grandchildren cried incessantly from hunger, but we couldn't find anything to feed them. All the money we had ran out, and food aid was very scarce.

My disabled son, Yazan Ziad Al-Hilu, fled with us. He has been disabled since birth due to an oxygen and potassium deficiency. My son Saheer passed away shortly before the war due to a lack of immunity and being afflicted with muscular dystrophy.

My disabled son Yazan has been admitted to Nasser Hospital six times due to his deteriorating health, caused by the poor environment in the shelters. His condition has worsened due to inhaling smoke from the fire we used for cooking. Now, after several days,

RAISING MY MARTYRED SON'S CHILDREN | 125

his condition has deteriorated significantly, as his body is struggling to tolerate the poor health, environmental, and nutritional conditions we have been living in since the first day of the Israeli occupation's war on the Gaza Strip.

Currently, I am taking care of my son Yazan, who needs special food. He needs meat and chicken to strengthen his body and resist disease, as he was accustomed to before the war. However, I can't find the appropriate food for him, and Yazan's health is deteriorating significantly every day. I fear losing my second son due to the occupation's unjust policies against us. These policies slowly and deliberately kill the people of Gaza.

My son Haitham and his two children, Ziad and Saheer, fled with us to Khan Younis. Haitham's elder son, Ziad, is 11 years old, and his younger son, Saheer, is ten years old. Haitham divorced and remarried before the war.

When the occupation forces besieged the area where we had taken refuge in the shelters, they demanded through loudspeakers that we leave the school. They managed to evacuate my disabled son, but we couldn't leave, so we remained in the school amid shelling, destruction, and heavy gunfire.

My son Haitham left the school with two other displaced people to get some food and water for us. We were living under siege inside the school and ran out of food and drink. After they left the school, an occupation tank shelled them, martyring my son Haitham and two other young men instantly on February 3, 2024.

Haitham left before noon, and I lost him between afternoon and sunset. I went out searching for him and found him lying on the ground, being eaten by cats. I couldn't bury him on the first day of his martyrdom due to Israeli shelling. On the second day, a group of displaced people went out with me, and we brought him back. The shelling had separated my son's head from his body, and I buried him in the cemetery of Khan Younis.

After burying my son Haitham, my husband, my disabled son, my two orphaned grandchildren, and I went to the Ja'ouni UNRWA school-turned-shelter in the Nuseirat refugee camp. Nuseirat camp has become a haven for thousands of displaced people. The harsh journey of displacement worsened my husband's health conditions; he suffers from heart attacks, high blood pressure, and diabetes, and he has a blood clot in his foot.

My son Haitham's martyrdom left me with his two children. My son Mohammed was also martyred, leaving me with his two daughters, Nasreen, one-and-a-half years old, and Celine, three months old. My granddaughter Celine was born in extremely difficult conditions during the war, enduring hardships during our displacement journey which has continued for almost eight consecutive months.

Celine suffers from malnutrition due to the lack of proper nutrition for her and her mother. We try to provide some milk for her, but there is no milk in Gaza, and we struggle to find even a little. We also face difficulty in providing diapers for the baby. Poor child! She was born in war and has lived through difficult conditions, yet she continues to fight for survival.

Also living with me is my disabled son Yazan, 13 years old, and my daughter Hanadi, who is married to Mohammed Sabehi. My daughters Rawida and Dina also live with me. Rawida's husband, Ramy Shaheiber, was martyred in a bombing in Gaza City. My sick husband also lives with us, along with several of our displaced relatives. The war has imposed difficult living conditions on all of us, conditions we never expected to experience.

My son Haitham worked in the field of automotive electricity, but he lost his job during the war and then lost his life. The war deprived me of him, his brother Mohammed, my daughter's husband Ramy, and many of my relatives who were killed by the Israeli war machine without mercy or compassion.

We live in shelters under difficult living conditions, without any money. The children need food and drink, and we struggle to provide even a little. There is no work in Gaza, and we have no means to sustain ourselves. We lost our home to the occupation forces' shelling, and I lost my sons. I try to take care of the orphaned children, who are entrusted to me.

We live in great hardship in the school-turned-shelter. We have no drinking water, and no water for washing clothes or for using in the bathroom. We have no comfort at all, and we have no privacy inside the school. The men live in tents in the schoolyard, while women and children sleep collectively in classrooms.

We haven't sat at one table as a family since the beginning of the war. We lost all the atmosphere of Ramadan; we didn't feel the coming or ending of Ramadan at all. We didn't feel the joy of Eid.

We suffer from poor hygiene due to water shortages and a severe shortage of clothes. It's hard for me to ask for help from anyone. We used to live a decent life, and now we rely on aid.

The children long for fruits and meat, but we don't have the money to buy them. Also, prices have skyrocketed during this war – more than ten times their pre-war prices. Often, my orphaned grandchildren go to sleep without having dinner. I walk long distances every day to search for bread and some food, but I can't find any. My sons used to own a car repair workshop, but now we suffer greatly, like all the displaced people, during the war.

My martyred son Haitham used to take care of all our affairs because of his father's illness, and after his martyrdom, we have lost our primary support. After all of this, we trust that Allah will not forsake us, He will not abandon us, He will grant us victory over the occupation, and all the injustice we face will disappear. I know that the pain will remain in our hearts as long as we live, but my dream now is for the war to end, to return to my home and rebuild it again, and for my Lord to grant me the strength to raise my orphaned grandchildren, educate them well, and protect them as they are the trust of my martyred sons. ♦

The Israeli Occupation Steals the Dreams of Palestinian Students

Mohammed Altaweel

> ❝ Three years ago, I began working toward my dream of enrolling in university and studying the English language, which I love. I reached the third level, and I only had one year left until I obtained my bachelor's degree in English from Al-Aqsa University. But the Israeli war stopped everything in Gaza. The occupation bombed and destroyed universities and schools, depriving us of our right to education. ❞

I COMPLETED high school several years ago, but due to financial circumstances, I couldn't continue to university. I taught myself

THE OCCUPATION STEALS THE DREAMS OF STUDENTS | 129

to be a hairdresser, and worked as a barber in several salons in the Bureij refugee camp. I managed to save some money and enrolled in Al-Aqsa University three years ago, majoring in the English language. I reached the third level, until the Israeli war on Gaza deprived all students of education, robbing us of an entire academic year.

The war not only deprived us of our right to continue education, but forced all students to waste a whole academic year, which in turn forced me to return to being a barber. I haven't cut hair since the beginning of my university education. I used to give private English lessons to students, and I was happy because I had managed to enroll in university and was close to achieving my dream. But the bombing, killing, destruction, and displacement that the people of Gaza have endured has now been our only situation for almost eight months straight.

Our house is in Block 12 in Bureij camp, in the middle of the Gaza Strip. I live there with my family of seven, including my brother and his wife. My father used to work inside the occupied Palestinian territories, known among Palestinians as "Israeli workers," but since the beginning of the Second Al-Aqsa Intifada in 2000, the occupation has deprived Gaza residents of work and canceled all their work permits, leaving my father unemployed. We only survive on the aid we receive from UNRWA every few months.

My family has endured difficult living conditions. My father couldn't find work. All the men in Gaza suffer from a lack of job opportunities due to the ongoing Israeli blockade on the Gaza Strip, which has lasted more than 18 years. The repeated Israeli wars on the Gaza Strip have also caused extensive damage to the economy, harmed employers, and greatly reduced job opportunities in the private sector.

The occupation had bombed dozens of houses adjacent to ours since the beginning of its war on Gaza on October 7, 2023, but we didn't leave our house. My father insisted that we stay and not go to live in tents. But then the Israeli forces announced the invasion of the central governorate camps in Gaza and issued warning notices asking us to evacuate to Deir al-Balah city. The neighborhood we lived in was invaded by the occupation forces. We were forced to flee and live in tents in Deir al-Balah city in the middle of the Gaza Strip.

Unwillingly, we left our house after the intensification of the Israeli shelling on Bureij camp. In Bureij camp, the occupation had destroyed large residential squares during the first two months of the war. We love our home; my father built it with great difficulty. But the occupation forced us out of it with the power of intense aerial bombardment. We left our home hoping to return to it soon. We didn't know then that we would never be able to return to it as it was destroyed by the occupation.

The occupation forces continued to invade the camps in the middle of the Gaza Strip for about a month – the period we spent in displacement tents. We followed the news daily, and learned that the occupation had caused unprecedented destruction in Bureij camp. After their withdrawal, we returned to our house, but found it demolished. The occupation forces had demolished our house, and all neighboring houses. We found nothing but rubble. The occupation's machinery drastically changed the landscape of our neighborhood and destroyed dozens of houses during its incursion into Bureij camp, killing and injuring hundreds.

When we left our house to escape the Israeli airstrikes, we thought we would only have to live in tents for a short time. However, after our house was destroyed, the tent became our primary home, where nine of us would live. We've endured many difficult days during the winter; the rain was heavy, the cold was extreme, and there were insect infestations.

We lived in tents in Deir al-Balah for a month. After the Israeli forces withdrew from the camps in the central Gaza Strip – Bureij, Maghazi, and Nuseirat – we went to the Nuseirat camp. We are currently living in a tent inside an UNRWA school set up for displaced people in the middle of Nuseirat.

Life in the tent is very difficult; there is no food to eat, and no water. Environmental pollution has spread widely, and waste is scattered everywhere. Municipalities can't transport waste to other places. We use public bathrooms, which are used by thousands of other displaced people living inside the school.

We thought we were safe inside the school, but Israeli forces have bombed the school twice. Our tent is in the schoolyard, and the Israeli airstrikes have targeted the schoolyard very close to our tent. But thankfully, we have been spared from the bombing, although dozens of displaced people inside the school have been killed or injured.

My family, like all Palestinian families in Gaza, has suffered from the many Israeli massacres during this war, the longest war on the Palestinian people – the most painful and destructive war. My uncle's wife was martyred in an Israeli airstrike in the early days of the war. The occupation bombed my aunt's house during the first month of the war, and most of those in the house, mostly children and displaced people, were martyred. The occupation also bombed the house of our family elders in Nuseirat. Abu Al-Saeed and more than 30 women, children, and elders were martyred in the bombing.

The bodies of our family remained under the rubble for several days, as there is little equipment in Gaza to extract bodies, and the occupation completely stopped the entry of fuel during the first two months of the war. The central governorate relied on only one machine to extract bodies and search for the missing, serving the more than 300,000 Palestinians living in the camps in the central Gaza Strip. After a week of bombing, our turn came. We retrieved all the bodies and buried them in mass graves in the camp.

My aunt's husband was injured in an Israeli airstrike during the war. He had been suffering from chronic diabetes for a while, and was receiving regular treatment. Due to the injury, he suffered major complications, and gangrene spread throughout his body. He was martyred due to his injury after the occupation deprived him of his right to treatment.

The war forced me to return to working as a barber. I had left that job three years ago when I started university. But now, I'm compelled to work in this profession to help my family with their expenses. We only receive one food assistance package every week to ten days, which isn't sufficient. Moreover, prices in the markets have increased significantly, more than tenfold what they were before the war.

I took my barber tools with me when we left our house. I worked as a barber during our stay in the displacement tents in Deir al-Balah city, and then continued working in the school set up for displaced people in Nuseirat camp. I wake up early every morning, sit at a small table in the schoolyard, and provide haircuts to displaced people.

Before the war, haircut prices varied, but I've significantly reduced the pricing now. Haircuts for children aged seven to 14 are priced at three Israeli shekels [.80 USD], while for adults, it's only five shekels [1.34 USD], and haircuts with a beard trim are priced at only eight shekels [2.14 USD]. I feel it's my duty to stand by the people and not exploit them in these difficult circumstances. I provide haircuts to around eight people daily, and while the money I earn is not enough to provide my family with a single meal, it covers the necessities for our tent, which has now become our home.

Three years ago, I began working toward my dream of enrolling in university and studying the English language, which I love. I reached the third level, and I only had one year left until I obtained my bachelor's degree in English from Al-Aqsa University. But the Israeli war stopped everything in Gaza. The occupation bombed and destroyed universities and schools, depriving us of our right to education.

My dream is for the war to end soon, and for us to rebuild our house and return to living in Bureij camp, where I was born, raised, and spent my childhood and youth. I hope students can return to their schools soon, and that the Ministry of Education can find a way to salvage the academic year we lost.

I am now working as a barber because of the circumstances of the war. I left the school desks due to the occupation's policy aimed at impoverishing Gaza's residents and destroying life in all aspects of the Gaza Strip. We live in a tragic and painful reality in Gaza. But what we've witnessed and experienced in this war, we haven't seen throughout all our lives. The war must stop, psychological support must be provided to Gaza's children, reconstruction must happen as soon as possible, and the occupation must be held accountable for all the genocidal crimes it has been committing for almost eight consecutive months. ♦

Birth and Death Under Israeli Bombs

Hajj Abu Sultan

> ❝ I can only walk with the help of a wooden crutch, but I asked my relatives to allow me to bury my wife, sons, and grandchildren. My tears flowed heavily as I placed soil over the bodies of my loved ones, my hands following my tears. I couldn't bear to complete their burial, so my relatives pulled me out and tried to calm me, but no words or expressions could alleviate my grief and pain, as my loss is too great for words to contain. ❞

As the Israeli war has intensified on the Gaza Strip, especially in the northern area and in Gaza City, thousands of families have been forced to flee from the north to the central and southern parts of Gaza. Among the families forced to flee was my son's wife's family. After they fled during the war, they lived with us in our house in Nuseirat refugee camp in central Gaza. My home is located in the midst of a cluster of UNRWA schools, which prompted many of our relatives, who considered the area safe, to seek refuge with us. We live south of the Gaza Valley, which the occupation classified as a safe area. However, on Saturday afternoon, February 17, 2024, the occupation forces bombed my house with several missiles, resulting in the complete destruction of my house and the martyrdom of ten of my family members, most of whom were women and children.

At 58, with so many members of my family taken from me, I must complete the remainder of my life with what's left of my family.

I am a sick man suffering from blood cancer. I have been suffering from the disease for several years, and have undergone intensive treatment sessions to control and limit its spread in my body. However, during the war I have lost my immunity and become susceptible to the simplest of diseases, which has forced me to leave my job and kept me from moving too much.

I used to go from my home to the mosque and then to visit my daughters and relatives. That was my life.

I married my soulmate, Ahlam Mohammed Abu Sultan, in 1987. She is from the town of Hamama, which was occupied in 1948. My marriage to her was a gift. We have three sons, Nabil, Mohammed, and Ahmed, and six daughters, Falastine, Fidaa, Reem, Noor Al-Huda, Aya, and Mina. Four of my daughters got married, and one of my sons got married. God blessed me with nine grandchildren from my daughters and my son Mohammed. I lived the most beautiful of days with them, and my wife and I were happy with what we had achieved for our children. We got to see them grow up, get married, and we were able to witness our grandchildren before our deaths. My wife was my biggest supporter throughout my illness, and the crutch who I leaned on at all times.

The occupation killed my two infant grandchildren. My middle son, Mohammed, got married on March 1, 2023, to a woman named Sajaa Al-Mamlouk. Mohammed's wife was five months pregnant when the war broke out and she suffered greatly. She gave birth to my granddaughter, Jouri, on January 27, 2024. We couldn't celebrate her arrival due to the intensity of the war and Israeli bombardment.

Jouri is my first granddaughter from my sons. We had planned a big celebration for her arrival. Before the war, my wife and I agreed to buy a cake and invite our relatives and friends to the party. But the occupation ruined everything we planned, and destroyed the joy of welcoming our granddaughter.

My daughter Reem married a man named Alaa Issa and gave birth to a baby boy named Ahmed. They were happy with the birth of their first child. But during the bombing, my daughter's husband, Alaa, and their infant son, Ahmed, were killed, along with the wife of my son, Sajaa Al-Mamlouk, and their infant daughter, Jouri. The occupation robbed us of our joy and deprived us of all our loved ones.

My granddaughter Jouri was two months old when she was killed, and my grandson Ahmed was five months old. They were born during the war and died during the war. We couldn't obtain birth certificates for them because all government facilities in Gaza are closed. We only have birth notifications for them. Now, we will obtain death certificates for them instead of birth certificates.

I have no dreams left after the departure of my wife, Ahlam.

My marriage to Ahlam made me one of the happiest people. Our marriage was the beginning of a beautiful future, and with her, I had managed to achieve my dreams. She was beautiful in every aspect, loved by everyone, and had a good relationship with everyone she knew. She never hurt anyone; she had a pure heart. Israeli bombs deprived us of her company.

My wife and I dreamed of seeing our eldest son, Nabil, 33, married. My wife searched a lot for a bride, and we were close to arranging his marriage, but the war prevented us from celebrating this. I told her that the first thing we would do after the war would be to finalize Nabil's marriage. The occupation ruined this dream. The occupation killed Nabil and killed my wife when our home was bombed.

Nabil was kind to me and his mother. He chose to delay his marriage so that he could work and support my wife and I. His younger brother married before him, and he was happy with that. He worked as a salesman in a grocery store in Nuseirat camp and he had memorized the Quran at the nearby mosque.

Nabil would give all his money to his mother. He would tell her to use it for household expenses. He cared more about our welfare than his own. I wished to rejoice with him and marry him off. I wished to live to see the day when I could embrace Nabil's children and play with them. Instead, I embraced Nabil as a martyr and buried him with my own hands in the soil. There are no words that can describe the great tragedy and sadness that the occupation has caused me and my daughters.

The martyrs in my family are my wife, Ahlam, my sons Nabil and Mohammed, my infant granddaughter Jouri, the wife of my son Sajaa Al-Mamlouk, the husband of my daughter Alaa Issa and their infant son, Ahmed, as well as the brothers of my son's wife, Abdullah and Malik Al-Mamlouk, and Iyad Abu Hatab. They were civilians who sought refuge in my house, fleeing from the bombardment. But the occupation's rockets pursued and killed them in what they thought was a safe place.

My son Mohammed was seriously injured in the bombing. He woke up a few days before his martyrdom and learned of the martyrdom of his mother, brother, wife, daughter, and relatives. He lived ten days of regret, pain, and despair in the intensive care unit, then he passed away from his injuries and was buried next to his wife and daughter.

Some of us survived.

We couldn't find enough open space in the cemetery to bury the martyrs, so we dug holes on top of the graves of our relatives who had passed away earlier, and buried our martyrs in the same spot. I can only walk with the help of a wooden crutch, but I asked my relatives to allow me to bury my wife, sons, and grandchildren. My tears flowed heavily as I placed soil over the bodies of my loved ones, my hands following my tears. I couldn't bear to complete their burial, so my relatives pulled me out and tried to calm me, but no words or expressions could alleviate my grief and pain, as my loss is too great for words to contain.

The occupation bombed my house while I was visiting my mother to give her medication. My daughter Manar was playing near her uncle's house with her friends, so she survived the bombing of my house. And my son Mohammed's mother-in-law was at the market with her daughters, so they survived the bombing. But my son Mohammed's mother-in-law's sons were at my house and were martyred.

My daughter Reem was in the kitchen preparing a bottle of milk for her infant son Ahmed when the bombing occurred. She suffered various injuries, and her infant son and husband were martyred. The occupation killed her hungry infant son; his mother wanted to feed him, but the occupation deprived her of that opportunity and wiped out her entire family.

My daughter Aya, 17 years old, was injured in the bombing. She suffered tissue damage, a tear duct rupture, and fainting in her left eye. She also suffered facial deformities, injuries to her eyelid and lip, bruises and fractures in her foot, knee, and other parts of her body, and underwent multiple surgeries. She still needs further surgeries outside of Gaza.

Many animals were also killed in the Israeli bombing. We owned many sheep and birds, but only one bird, which my son Nabil had bought before the war, survived the bombing. I will never slaughter it. It's a memento of my martyred son, and I will continue to take great care of it.

My son Nabil was injured before his martyrdom in a previous bombing that targeted a neighboring house where he worked. He suffered a pelvic fracture.

We lost our family and our home. Now, I live with my young daughters Reem, Aya, Manar, and my son Ahmed in my elderly mother's house. We have no real shelter. We fled, like all the residents of Gaza, during the Israeli forces' invasion. We fled from Nuseirat camp to Rafah. We have now returned to Nuseirat camp.

All I wish and dream for is for the war to stop, for the Israeli forces to be held accountable for their crimes, for the world to be just to us and restore our occupied land, and for the reconstruction of the Gaza Strip to be expedited so that we can live the remainder of our lives in dignified homes. ♦

Only My Brother and I Survived the Bombing of Our Home

Hala Adel Al-Najmi

❝ Our life in the shelter is difficult. Every day, I have to go up and down the stairs many times which is very difficult with my injuries. I need to travel with my brother Kareem to receive treatment, which has caused me severe knee pain. We have to get water and food ourselves because everyone living with us in the school is facing similarly difficult living conditions to what we've been through. ❞

ON Monday, December 11, 2023, I was asleep in our crowded house in Maghazi refugee camp in the middle of the Gaza Strip.

ONLY MY BROTHER AND I SURVIVED | 141

We woke up for Fajr prayer, and suddenly, our house was subjected to intense shelling. I lost consciousness, and hours later I woke up to find myself in the hospital, with serious injuries all over my body.

My name is Hala Adel Al-Najmi, and I am 13 years old. I am from the Maghazi refugee camp in the middle of the Gaza Strip. I lived a beautiful life before the start of the war. Since the first day of the war, our house has been turned into a refuge for many displaced people who've fled from the Israeli shelling that has targeted all areas of the Gaza Strip. We lived together with the displaced people as one family, sharing with them everything we had. I had hoped that the war would end without us being harmed, but the war has been ongoing now for several months, and I cannot describe the pain caused to me by the Israeli occupation. This pain will haunt me for the rest of my life.

While my family was praying, the occupation forces bombed our house. The force of the explosion threw me and my brother Kareem, 20 years old, into the street behind our house. My brother Kareem and I were the only ones to survive the bombing – everyone else was martyred.

I woke up after several hours to find myself in the hospital, and immediately asked about my family. I was told that they were receiving treatment at the hospital in Rafah, in the south of the Gaza Strip, while my brother Kareem and I were receiving treatment at the Al-Aqsa Martyrs Hospital in Deir al-Balah. I was informed that my brother Kareem's injuries were all over his body, and that he had lost bone and flesh from his left foot. I was told that he was receiving treatment in a ward adjacent to the one where I was receiving treatment.

I requested to see my dear brother Kareem to check on him, but when I saw him, I was greatly shocked. I couldn't recognize him due to the severity of his injuries. His injuries were extensive, resulting in burns and significant disfigurement all over his body. The bombing caused burns on his face. I was hesitant to hold his hand and greet him, but I was relieved that he was still alive.

I stayed in the Al-Aqsa Martyrs Hospital for three months receiving treatment. For a month and a half, I was in a wheelchair and unable to walk. I had suffered deep wounds all over my body, and the doctors performed skin grafting on my hands. The bombing caused nerve damage in my left hand, and I underwent surgery every three days. I underwent about 16 surgeries at Al-Aqsa Martyrs Hospital.

After completing my treatment at Al-Aqsa Martyrs Hospital, and after undergoing many surgeries, I was transferred to a hospital in Khan Younis city for neurological physical therapy for my legs. I couldn't walk for over three weeks.

My brother Khalid is married and lives in an apartment outside our house. He survived the bombing and death. I went to his house after the invasion of Khan Younis city, when I was suffering from injuries all over my body. I cried a lot because of my longing for my family, but I didn't know about their martyrdom yet.

After the bombing intensified in Deir al-Balah, we decided to evacuate to Rafah city. We rode a truck in the middle of the night, amid danger and heavy bombing, to Rafah city. We lived in tents in the Shabura area in Rafah for 13 days. During this time, I had a fever, and my wounds caused me a lot of pain. I suffered from severe infections in my body, and I couldn't find any treatment or pain relief.

After 13 days of living in tents, and due to my poor health condition, the people of Rafah hosted us in a small shop where dozens of families were staying. We stayed there for two weeks, and after the end of the occupation's invasion in the central camps, we went to my uncle's house in Maghazi camp.

My uncle's house is adjacent to our house. It is basically uninhabitable from the damage due to the bombing of our house. We all slept in one room there. I lived there for 12 days. After that, I moved with my brother to shelters. We faced difficulty in getting food, drink, cleaning materials, clothes, and everything else.

I constantly asked about my father, mother, and siblings, and my relatives kept telling me that my family was fine and was receiving treatment in Rafah city. But I started feeling like my relatives weren't telling me the truth, and my worry and fear for my family increased every day. My relatives' looks toward me were strange; I felt like they were hiding something from me, but they insisted my family was fine and receiving treatment.

I was playing on my brother's wife's phone, and I opened the pictures on the phone. I found a picture with the names of my father and mother and the date of their martyrdom, December 11, 2023. I was greatly shocked – I couldn't believe what I saw. I cried a lot, but I still didn't know anything about my siblings.

I thought the bombing had only led to the martyrdom of my father and mother, but after pleading with my brother's wife, she finally told me that everyone in the house was martyred, and only my brother Kareem and I had survived. My father, Adel Al-Najmi, 52 years old, and my mother, Mona, 46 years old, were martyred, along with my brother Eyad, 29 years old, and his infant daughter, Hoor, 6 months old.

Also martyred were my brother Jamal, 27 years old, my brother Mohammed, 21 years old, my sister Ala'a, 26 years old, and her son, the child Joud Maqdad, seven years old. My sister's young husband, Amjad Maher Maqdad, 28 years old, was also martyred. Everyone in our house was martyred, and dozens of our neighbors were injured. My neighborhood was completely destroyed.

At the beginning of January 2024, after the occupation forces invaded Maghazi camp, we fled first to Deir al-Balah city and then to Nuseirat camp. Now, we are living in a school-turned-shelter for displaced people run by UNRWA in Nuseirat camp. I have never felt safe for a single moment inside the school.

The occupation forces bombed the school several times, and dozens of displaced people were martyred and injured in the school bombings. My brother's wife was going to get some food when she was hit by shrapnel from the occupation's rockets bombing the schoolyard. Doctors described her injury as moderate.

Our life in the shelter is difficult. Every day, I have to go up and down the stairs many times which is very difficult with my injuries.

I need to travel with my brother Kareem to receive treatment, which has caused me severe knee pain. We have to get water and food ourselves because everyone living with us in the school is facing similarly difficult living conditions to what we've been through.

All the places inside the Al-Aqsa Martyrs Hospital, where I stayed, were filled with beds for the injured. The number of injuries coming to the hospital daily was very high, far exceeding the hospital's capacity. The occupation's crimes have not stopped for a moment since the beginning of the war.

I dream that the war will end soon, and that I can live with my brother again. I hope my brother can walk and move his hand again. We don't feel any aspect of the life we used to live, yet we must continue after losing everything. I hope to travel with my brother to complete our treatment. My brother Kareem currently cannot walk. My dream is for him to stand on his feet and continue his life better than he was before.

I still need treatment. The stitches in my body hurt me, and my body temperature often rises to 40°C [104°F]. I can't find painkillers or treatment for my injury. We don't have food or water.

I miss my school. I am an excellent student, but I lost my academic certificates in the bombing of our house. I lost everything.

I miss my classmates. I miss studying. I miss my life before the war. I miss coming back from school and finding my mother preparing food. I miss eating together. But my mother was martyred. The occupation killed her and left me to continue my life without her.

The war must end immediately. The occupation must be held accountable for all the crimes it has committed against us in Gaza during the genocidal war it has been waging on the Gaza Strip for almost eight consecutive months. ◆

Remember Us

Paul Catafago

Please
remember us.
Remember we were known
for our generosity
and our creativity.

Remember
we valued song and poetry.

Remember
that our culture esteemed writers,
teachers and farmers.

Remember
we did not idolize material
or money.

Remember though
we were a people who worshipped
the creator in different ways,
and believed in different theologies,
we practiced tolerance and acceptance
of the other.

Remember
we were a people who valued friendship and family.
and if you became our friend
you were a member of our family.

Remember
that in our houses there were
four generations who lived.

Remember
we were a people who honoured
both our elders and our children

Remember
when you entered our houses
we asked you if you were hungry.

Remember
the food we made for you;
that you had never seen so much food;
that it was all so delicious.

Remember that before we ate,
regardless of our religion,
we thanked the creator
and we did the same
after we finished eating.

Remember our land;
how we cherished and tended to it,
understanding it as a gift of the creator.

Remember
the orange groves and
the pomegranate trees.
Remember you helped,
harvest our olive trees in the fall.

Remember

Remember
our joy; our embroidery;
our culture of poetry.

Remember
how much we loved life,
how we regarded every day a blessing.

Remember

They will tell you lies about us now.
They will have you judge
us by the actions of a few.

They will not tell you
why some of us were rendered mad
when our lands were stolen.

They will say we are evil.
They will say we are terrorists.
Some will say we are not even human;
not worthy of basic rights.

They will kill our children
and justify the killings.

They will do horrific things
to us and never be held accountable.

And you will become weary.

But remember.

Remember
who we are and
where we come from.

Remember
our light, our generosity and our love.
Remember our dignity.

So in these difficult times,
as we are in deep grief
mourning the deaths of
more than 17,000 of our people,
more than 5,000 children,
stand with us,
grieve with us.
Then struggle for justice with us.

Read our poems.
Eat our foods.
Wear clothes with
our embroidery.

Bear witness to
who you know us to be.

Remember how
when you came and stayed with us,
we laughed so much and
how much we loved life.

So remember all of that;
and do not pity us now.
Just stand with us and
remember
who we were
and who we will always be.

Remember
our strength and our resolve.

Remember
we taught you a word in Arabic
that is particular to our people,
Sumud
which means steadfastness.
Remember
our Sumud,
how steadfast we are.

Remember
when you left us,
we told you to come back, to return.

Remember.
We too shall return.

Remember we shall return.

Paul Catafago is a US-based poet and cultural organizer whose family has been part of the movement for self-determination in Palestine since before 1948. "Remember Us," which was nominated for a 2025 "Best of the Net Award," was first published in Singapore Unboud's Suspect *journal in December 2023. It is included in Paul's book of poems,* Sumud: Poems of the Palestinian Diaspora, *Sligo Creek Publishing, 2024.*

Acknowledgments

We would like to express our gratitude to the 27 families who shared their stories in this book. Our special thanks go to Jennifer Bing, the National Director of the US Palestine Activism Program at the American Friends Service Committee, for her valuable feedback and edits, which made this book a reality. We would also like to express our appreciation to the exiled Palestinian poet Paul Catafago for contributing his poem "Remember Us," which provides a poignant end to this collection of stories of the displaced.

About Haymarket Books

Haymarket Books is a radical, independent, nonprofit book publisher based in Chicago. Our mission is to publish books that contribute to struggles for social and economic justice. We strive to make our books a vibrant and organic part of social movements and the education and development of a critical, engaged, and internationalist left.

We take inspiration and courage from our namesakes, the Haymarket Martyrs, who gave their lives fighting for a better world. Their 1886 struggle for the eight-hour day—which gave us May Day, the international workers' holiday—reminds workers around the world that ordinary people can organize and struggle for their own liberation. These struggles—against oppression, exploitation, environmental devastation, and war—continue today across the globe.

Since our founding in 2001, Haymarket has published more than nine hundred titles. Radically independent, we seek to drive a wedge into the risk-averse world of corporate book publishing. Our authors include Angela Y. Davis, Arundhati Roy, Keeanga-Yamahtta Taylor, Eve Ewing, Aja Monet, Mariame Kaba, Naomi Klein, Rebecca Solnit, Mohammed El-Kurd, José Olivarez, Noam Chomsky, Winona LaDuke, Robyn Maynard, Leanne Betasamosake Simpson, Howard Zinn, Mike Davis, Marc Lamont Hill, Dave Zirin, Astra Taylor, and Amy Goodman, among many other leading writers of our time. We are also the trade publishers of the acclaimed Historical Materialism Book Series.

Haymarket also manages a vibrant community organizing and event space in Chicago, Haymarket House, the popular Haymarket Books Live event series and podcast, and the annual Socialism Conference.

Also Available from Haymarket Books

After Savagery
Gaza, Genocide, and the Illusion of Western Civilization
Hamid Dabashi

Heaven Looks Like Us: Palestinian Poetry
Edited by George Abraham and Noor Hindi

Light in Gaza: Writings Born of Fire
Edited by Jehad Abusalim, Jennifer Bing,
and Mike Merryman-Lotze

Palestine in a World on Fire
Katherine Natanel and Ilan Pappé

Perfect Victims: And the Politics of Appeal
Mohammed El-Kurd

Their Borders, Our World: Building New Solidarities with Palestine
Edited by Mahdi Sabbagh

Visualizing Palestine
A Chronicle of Colonialism and the Struggle for Liberation
Edited by Jessica Anderson, Aline Batarseh, and Yosra El Gazzar
Created by Visualizing Palestine